MONTACUTE HOUSE

Somerset

Malcolm Rogers

THE NATIONAL TRUST

This account of Montacute and its contents is greatly indebted to its predecessors by Dr Mark Girouard (1961) and Dudley Dodd (1978); to Jim Phelips for his invaluable researches on the Phelips family and for permission to publish the 1782 Survey researched by his son-in-law Robert Pearce RIBA; and to the staff of the Somerset County Record Office for making available information from the Phelips Papers which they hold. Rebecca S. More has put at my disposal the results of her researches on the early history of the family. For their help in a variety of ways I wish to thank at the National Trust: Anthony Mitchell, Historic Buildings Representative for the Wessex region; David Mounce, Administrator at Montacute, and his staff; Alastair Laing, Advisor on Paintings and Sculpture; and my patient editor, Oliver Garnett. Of my colleagues at the National Portrait Gallery, Julia King, Reyahn King, Maria Pacan, Bruce Irving, Terence Pepper and Shrutica Patel have given much needed support.

Malcolm Rogers

CONTENTS

Introduction   *page* 5

Chapter One Early history   6

Phelips family tree   8

Chapter Two The building of Montacute   11

Chapter Three The later Phelips family   18

Chapter Four The revival of Montacute   30

Chapter Five Tudor and Jacobean portraiture   34

Chapter Six The textiles   44

Plans of the house   50

Chapter Seven The house   52

Chapter Eight The garden, park and estate   84

Plan of the estate, *c.*1782   92

Appendix Inventories of the Library   93

Bibliography   94

Index   95

INTRODUCTION

That eccentric and indefatigable traveller Thomas Coryate of Odcombe, a village close by Montacute, recalls in his *Crudities. Hastily gobled up in Five Months Travells* (1611) his visit to Bonn, and the palace of the Archbishop of Cologne overlooking the Rhine which he was shown there. One of his travelling-companions asserted that England could not equal it, and Coryate replies with patriotic fervour that

besides many other English Palaces that do surpasse that of the Archbishop of Colen, there is one in mine owne country of Somersetshire, even the magnificent house of my most worthy and right Worshipful neighbour and Mecoenas, Sir Edward Phillippes . . . in the town of Montacute, so stately adorned with the statues of the nine Worthies, that may bee at the least equally ranked with this of Bonna, if not something preferred before it.

It is hard to appreciate the impact which a house like Montacute had when it was first built; it must have seemed wonderful beyond the dreams of most of those who lived nearby, a work of astonishing splendour and pride. Today time has softened the effect, and eyes are used to buildings on a huge scale. Nevertheless Montacute, its garden and park, retain an extraordinary power to stir the emotions.

The house was built in the last years of the sixteenth century by Sir Edward Phelips (1560?–1614), a successful lawyer, who first entered Parliament in 1584, became Speaker in 1604 and later Master of the Rolls and Chancellor to the household of Henry, Prince of Wales, heir to the throne. His architect was almost certainly the local mason William Arnold, whose documented buildings include Cranborne Manor, Dorset, and Wadham College, Oxford. The house which Phelips and Arnold built, of the warm stone from nearby Ham Hill, was the home of the Phelips family for more than three hundred years. It survives as one of the best preserved of Elizabethan mansions, and has been described as 'the most beautiful Elizabethan house in England'.

Naturally there have been changes over the years, most notably in the 1780s when Edward Phelips (1725–97) grafted on a new west front using ornamental stonework purchased from Clifton Maybank, a mid-sixteenth-century house near Yeovil. Internally, Montacute preserves much of its original decoration, but all the furnishings have long since vanished; indeed the house was virtually stripped of its contents in 1651, 1834 and again in 1929. In 1911 the Phelips family left Montacute to live in London, and the house was leased to a series of tenants, the most illustrious of whom was Lord Curzon, formerly Viceroy of India, who lived at Montacute, first with his mistress, the novelist Elinor Glyn, and subsequently with his second wife. In 1931 it was saved from demolition by the intervention of the Society for the Protection of Ancient Buildings, and presented to the National Trust by the generosity of Ernest Cook, grandson of the founder of the travel agents Thomas Cook. After the Second World War the Trust refurnished the house with the help of numerous loans and gifts – outstanding among these the bequest of tapestries, furniture and works of art from the industrialist Sir Malcolm Stewart – and restored the gardens and park. In 1975 the house became the first outstation of the National Portrait Gallery, and in the Long Gallery and adjoining rooms is an important display of historical portraits from the sixteenth and seventeenth centuries.

(Opposite page) The west front

CHAPTER ONE
EARLY HISTORY

The settlement of Montacute, dominated by the conical St Michael's Hill, has its origins in the estate known in the seventh century as Logworesbeorh, which William of Malmesbury in his *De Gestis Regum* linked with Logor, one of the original twelve monks of the Benedictine Glastonbury Abbey. At some time in the ninth century the name was changed to Bishopston, perhaps in connection with Tunbeorht, Abbot of Glastonbury and Bishop of Winchester, and a part of the main street of the present village still retains that name. According to legend, in the early eleventh century, when Tofig, King Cnut's standard-bearer, was lord there, the village sexton was told in a dream to dig on the hill above the village. This the villagers did, and

discovered a black flint carving of Christ crucified. Tofig gave this holy relic to the church of Waltham which he had founded on the edge of Epping Forest, and which later became the great abbey of Waltham Holy Cross. King Harold held this relic in especial veneration, and took 'Holy Cross' as his war-cry at the Battle of Hastings.

From the time of the Norman Conquest the village was known as Mountague, a name derived from the Latin for its distinctive hill, *mons acutus*. William the Conqueror granted the mount to his half-brother, Robert, Count of Mortain, who built a castle on the summit by 1068, the year in which it was besieged by English insurgents, who considered it an especially provocative symbol of Norman

Montacute takes its name from the pointed hill ('mons acutus' in Latin) to the south-west of the house. Now called St Michael's Hill, it is topped by a folly built by Edward Phelips in 1760

oppression on account of the hill's religious significance and association with King Harold. By the beginning of the twelfth century the castle had presumably ceased to have any military importance, as around 1102 William, Count of Mortain, Robert's successor, gave it to the Cluniac priory which he had founded in the village below. In 1192 King John, when Count of Mortain, gave the surrounding land to the monks of Montacute, and the manor remained in monastic hands until Henry VIII dissolved the monastery in 1539. Shortly after, the Crown leased the property to Henry's Secretary of State, Sir William Petre (Long Gallery, 8). The priory church was demolished almost immediately, and all that remains today is the gatehouse and dovecote, which lie on the opposite side of the village to Montacute House.

In 1542 Petre's lease was acquired by the courtier and poet Sir Thomas Wyatt of Allington in Kent, but fell to the Crown in 1554, following the attainder and execution of Wyatt's son, Sir Thomas the Younger, for leading the rebellion which bears his name. The lease reverted again to Petre, and remained in his possession until his death in 1572. In 1574 Robert Dudley, Earl of Leicester, acquired the lease to Montacute, but did not hold it long. The lease, and subsequently the manor itself, passed to the Freke family, and did not come into the hands of Sir Edward Phelips until 1608 – several years after he had built the house, the site of which had never belonged to the monastery.

The Phelips family had settled in the vicinity of Montacute at least seventy years before the dissolution of the priory. The first identifiable ancestor of the builder is his great-grandfather Thomas Phelips (d.1501). His origins are still shrouded in mystery, but there is some evidence that he came from Dorset. In 1460 he was living at Lufton, a mile to the east of Montacute and a manor owned by the Brooke family, Barons of Cobham in Kent, in whose household he may have held office. It was almost certainly the patronage of this powerful family which allowed him to rise from yeoman in 1460 to the rank of gentleman less than six years later, and to obtain the Crown appointment of escheator (handling property which had lapsed to the Crown) for the combined counties of Somerset

Sir William Petre, Henry VIII's Secretary of State, briefly held the lease of Montacute in the early 1540s; by Steven van der Meulen, 1567 (Long Gallery, 8)

and Dorset in 1471 and again in 1478. Between 1474 and 1480 he moved from Lufton to Montacute, and in 1479 he purchased a half-burgage (or rented property) in North Street, Montacute (which ran roughly on the line of the present main drive), 'between a burgage of Thomas Geffray and a garden of the said Thomas Phelips on the south'. Phelips made his will at Montacute on 1 January 1501, and directed that he should be buried in the priory, as distinct from the parish church, perhaps suggesting that he may have performed some administrative function for the monastery. In his will he left all his burgages, lands and tenements in Montacute to Jane, his wife, and to her heirs in perpetuity. A little later in 1501 John, Lord Cobham, granted to Jane Phelips a lease of his manor of Brooke Montacute, a little north of the village.

Thomas's eldest son, Richard, was born about 1480. In 1507 he was appointed Under-Sheriff for Somerset, and in 1509 attended the funeral of Henry VII and the coronation of Henry VIII as a member

THE PHELIPS FAMILY

The owners of Montacute House are shown in CAPITALS

*denotes subjects of portraits at Montacute House

†denotes members of the family with monuments in St. Catherine's Church

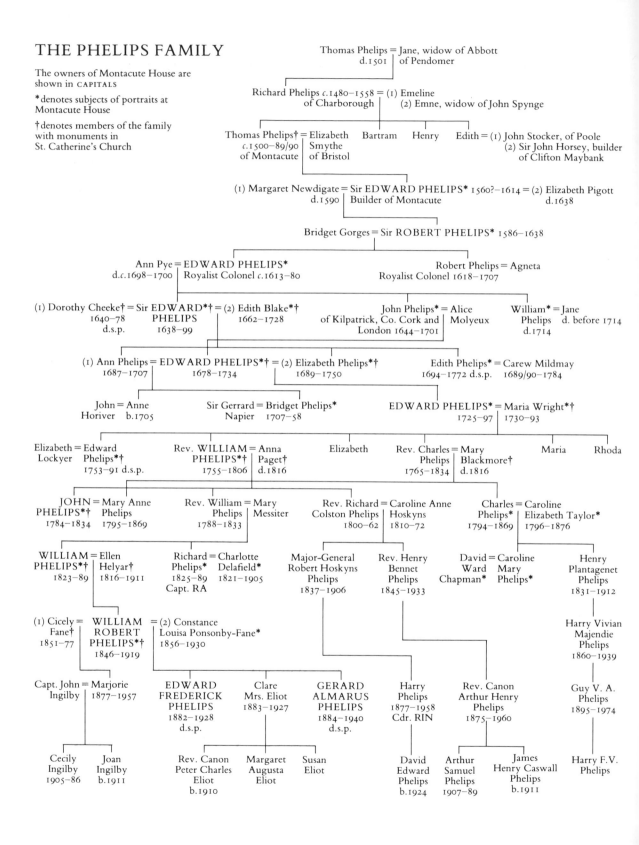

of the King's guard. Between 1511 and 1516 he was Deputy-Controller of wine imports through the ports of Lyme and Weymouth, and in 1512 he was returned to Parliament as one of the two burgesses for Poole. Between 1522 and 1528 he leased the entire toll or customs of Poole, which controlled also Lyme and Weymouth, and had considerable trouble in satisfying the Exchequer with his final accounts. In 1524 he was appointed Surveyor-General of the estates in the West Country of one of England's richest landowners, Cecily, Dowager Marchioness of Dorset, and of her son, Thomas Grey, 2nd Marquis, an appointment made, in the Marchioness's own words, 'having a special trust and confidence in one Richard Phelips, thinking him to be of just dealing, honest in behaviour and of good conscience'. Phelips organised an extensive survey of the Grey estates, but by his brisk and probably rapacious dealings he fell foul of his employer, who charged him with extortion and oppression of her tenants, claiming before the Star Chamber that Phelips and his second-in-command

The carved relief above the entrance to the west front celebrates the marriage of Sir John Horsey to Edith, daughter of Richard Phelips, and came originally from their home near Yeovil, Clifton Maybank

(a former associate of Cardinal Wolsey) had 'taken great sums of money and rewards which they have converted and employed to their own uses'. He nevertheless continued to work for the Grey family into the 1540s. In 1531 he took over management of the prestigious royal manor of Canford, and attended as a 'gentleman servitor' the coronation of Anne Boleyn in 1533.

Before 1514 Phelips had married Emily (or Emeline; nothing more is known of her), and the couple had in all four sons and two daughters. About 1515 Phelips is described as 'late of London, Montacute, Poole and Soutwark', and from about 1523 he, his wife and sons Thomas and Bartram are recorded as living at Sock Dennis in Tintinhull, a small manor on the old road from Ilchester to Montacute. He had, however, leased property in and around Poole from c.1515, and in October 1531 he moved to Charborough, north-west of Poole, as lessee of the manor. In the next ten years he bought both the manors of Corfe Mullen and Corfe Hubart nearby. He also apparently had property in Twickenham and Isleworth, near London. During his long and turbulent life, Phelips increased very considerably the standing of his family, both locally and nationally at court and as a parliamentarian.

Phelips made his will on 24 January 1557, thanking God for a long life and begging forgiveness for his sins. Masses were to be said for himself and his first wife (he had remarried shortly before his death) for six years. His sole executor was his son Thomas, and no mention is made of his other sons – Bartram, who perhaps died young, and Henry, the black sheep of the family, who, after being a student for twenty years, robbed his parents and fled to the Continent, where, among other misdeeds, he betrayed William Tyndale, author of the vulgate Bible, to the imperial authorities in Antwerp in 1535. Richard Phelips's daughter Edith was already well provided for, as she had first married one of the richest of Poole merchants, John Stocker, and secondly, after his death, Sir John Horsey, builder of Clifton Maybank, not far from Montacute. The latter marriage is commemorated on the west front of Montacute in the initials 'J' and 'EH' on a carved panel which once decorated Clifton Maybank (see Chapter Three).

When his father moved to Poole in 1531, Thomas Phelips (c.1500–89/90) continued to live at Sock Dennis. It was probably in the early 1520s that he married Elizabeth, daughter of Matthew Smythe of Bristol, and he had by her at least four sons. The families were to remain close for several generations. In his youth Thomas was evidently something of a tearaway, and his father's attempts to gain him a place in the household of Henry VIII's chief minister, Thomas Cromwell, were frustrated by his son's involvement in a prison escape at Ilchester in 1533. He nevertheless found employment with a number of prominent figures in the South West, notably Jane Seymour's brother, Sir Edward Seymour, who may have found him an appointment in the household of Catherine Parr on her marriage to Henry VIII in 1543. He represented West Country boroughs in Parliaments from 1545 to 1558, but thereafter played little part in public life. In his will, dated 25 September 1588, he asked to be buried without great ceremony, and, since he seems to have found his three eldest sons unsatisfactory, appointed his youngest son, Edward, sole executor, and left him his house at Montacute, on condition that he paid his eldest brother £650 for it.

Thomas Phelips's house in Montacute is said to have stood near the present stables, and was demolished in the later seventeenth century. Nothing is known of its appearance, though its presence flickers tantalisingly through one of Thomas Phelips's letters, in which he complains of the uncouth behaviour of his neighbour, George Speake (whose sister was married to his own eldest son):

[He] followed me through the hall, using these woordes, he would not leave me so. [I went] through the court into the Parlor where I doe customably rest and lye [he] ever contynueinge his prittle prattle, drave me for my quiettnes to goe up into the chamber over where I doe lie, you do knoe, the staires narrow and darke . . .

CHAPTER TWO

THE BUILDING OF MONTACUTE

Edward Phelips repaid his father's confidence in him. He trained as a lawyer and was called to the bar in 1579. Energetic and able, he soon made a great fortune, and like many successful men, gravitated to public life. He was elected Member of Parliament for various pocket boroughs outside Somerset between 1584 and 1596, and for Somerset in 1601. Two years later he was appointed Serjeant-at-Law and King's Serjeant, and, together with his eldest son, was knighted by James I. In November 1603 he took part in the trial of Sir Walter Ralegh, but did not share in 'the brutal manner' in which Sir Edward Coke prosecuted. The Speakership of the House of Commons followed in 1604. The King found him a compliant Speaker, and it was he who opened for the prosecution at the trial of Guy Fawkes after the Gunpowder Plot of 1605. His speech on this occasion survives, as also that for the opening of Parliament in 1604; both are dinosaurs of rhetoric. In 1610 he became Chancellor of the Duchy of Cornwall in the household of Henry, Prince of Wales, and in 1611 Master of the Rolls, an extremely lucrative post. As a judge he was considered 'over swift in judging', and like several of his family he was ferocious with Roman Catholics, on one occasion condemning a man to death 'simply for entertaining a Jesuit'. Prince Henry died sadly young in 1612, but Sir Edward remained in royal favour. He was responsible for organising the Masque of the Middle Temple, designed by Inigo Jones and held in the Great Hall of Whitehall Palace to celebrate the marriage of Henry's sister to the Elector Frederick in February 1613.

Sir Edward married twice: first, Margaret Newdigate from Haynes in Bedfordshire, by whom he had two sons, and secondly, Elizabeth Pigott from Doddershall in Buckinghamshire. Besides his mansion at Montacute, he had a town house in Broad Street in London, and rented from the Blunt family the great house at Wanstead in Essex, former home of Elizabeth I's favourites, the Earls of Leicester and Essex. There he entertained James I on several occasions. He died in 1614 and was buried at Montacute. No church monument was raised to him, nor is his place of burial marked, but the house which he built at Montacute remains as his secular memorial.

There is no documentary evidence of when Sir Edward began his new house, but the dates 1598 and 1599 are found in a stained-glass window and on a fireplace. The date 1601, carved over the east doorway, may well give the date when the house was completed, and we may hypothesise a building-period of ten years, giving a starting date *c.*1590. The earliest mention of the house is in William Camden's *Britannia* (1607), although Thomas Coryate of Odcombe, who published his account in 1611, must have known it from the first.

Phelips's architect was almost certainly the Somerset mason William Arnold. The main evidence for this is a letter of 10 February 1610 from Dorothy Wadham, who was responsible for Arnold's appointment as designer and builder of Wadham College, Oxford, to her brother Lord Petre, in which she writes that Arnold had been 'commended' to her by her 'good frend and lovinge neighboure Sr Edward Phelipps'. Supporting evidence comes from Cranborne Manor, Dorset, and Dunster Castle in Somerset, both of which contain architectural details out of the same workshop as details at Montacute. At both Cranborne and Dunster, Arnold is documented as the master mason in charge. In addition, the porch at Cranborne finds its twin at Wayford Manor in Somerset, where there is a fireplace which in its turn matches the fireplace in the Library (Great Chamber) at Montacute. Indeed, scattered over Dorset, Somerset, Wiltshire and Devon, are chimney-pieces, porches, tombs and so on, which tie in with Montacute, Cranborne and Dunster, and which testify to Arnold's productivity and probably also his influence in the region.

A certain amount is known of Arnold's life, but not as much as one would like. From at least 1595 he was living at Charlton Musgrove near Wincanton, and about 12 miles from Montacute. There his children were baptised, and there he served as a church warden. For some reason which has not been satisfactorily explained, he appears to have used two surnames and to have been called variously 'William Arnold', 'William Goverson' and 'William Arnold, alias Goverson'. Between about 1609 and 1610 he was responsible for remodelling Cranborne for Robert Cecil, Earl of Salisbury; from 1610 to 1613 he was in charge of the building of Wadham College, and in 1617 he undertook the remodelling of part of Dunster Castle for George Luttrell. He did not get on with

Sir Edward Phelips (1560?–1614), the builder of Montacute (Screens Passage)

William Arnold, the probable architect of Montacute, is known to have worked at Dunster Castle, also in Somerset, which contains similar architectural details; watercolour of the north front of Dunster in 1839, by John Buckler

Luttrell, who went to law with him for exceeding his estimates. Arnold died at Charlton Musgrove and was buried there on 12 March 1637.

Dorothy Wadham thought him 'an honest man' and 'a perfectt workman', and Sir Edward Hext, one of the Wadham trustees, said he was 'wonnderfully sought being in deede the absolutest and honestest workeman in Ingland'. George Luttrell, tight-lipped, had still to admit his 'great experience in architecture'. Arnold was, however, not an architect in the modern sense – such a figure hardly existed in Elizabethan England – but an artist-craftsman of a high order, and clearly a figure of unusual skill and imagination. He was by origin a stonemason and sculptor, and one of a family of craftsmen; Edmund and Thomas Arnold, perhaps his brothers, were both employed as masons at Wadham College, and as early as 1555 an Arnold Goverson (who seems to have been his father) is recorded as a joiner at Longleat in Wiltshire. Arnold stands, therefore, in the medieval tradition of working craftsmen who could also supply designs, and who were prepared to work hand-in-hand with clients who might well have ideas of their own, and, indeed, be architectural amateurs of distinction.

The part played by Phelips in the design of his new house remains mysterious, but it is worth noting that Montacute resembles in some respects representations of the slightly earlier house built by Phelips's brother-in-law, Sir Robert Newdigate, at Haynes, south of Bedford, notably in the disposition of the east court, its pavilions and gatehouse. It was presumably Phelips who pointed Arnold in this direction.

In the sixteenth century visitors approached the new house from the old main road between Montacute and Ilchester, which ran parallel to the east front of the house, through an outer court and then through a gatehouse into the east court. This gatehouse, which stood equidistant between the two surviving pavilions, has long since disappeared, but evidence suggests that it was a substantial building with lodgings, and it may have resembled the gatehouse at Burton Agnes Hall (1610) in Yorkshire, or the more whimsical one at Lanhydrock (finished in 1651) in Cornwall. The two pavilions with their ogee roofs, turrets and obelisks, give a clue to its appearance, though deprived of their chimney stacks by Lord Curzon. Gatehouse and pavilions were furnished as bedrooms in the 1638 inventory. The court was, as it remains today, bounded on south and north sides with a balustraded wall, crowned by obelisks, and punctuated at the centre by transparent rotundas with transparent

The east front, with its forecourt bounded by a balustraded wall and garden pavilions

and boldly top-heavy cupolas and finials. The overall effect is of an exquisite pastiche of the fortified forecourt of a medieval house.

On the west side of the court a flight of six steps leads up to the stone terrace immediately in front of the house. This is flanked on the east side by six free-standing Doric columns, now supporting electric lights, but originally topped by stone finials. From this terrace the house rises like a cliff. Though it lacks the bleak arrogance of Hardwick Hall in Derbyshire or the sheer flamboyance of Wollaton Hall in Nottinghamshire, it must nevertheless have seemed prodigious in the early seventeenth century. Certainly, it left an indelible impression on the mind of Thomas Coryate.

Montacute is built of oolitic limestone from nearby Ham Hill, notable for its warmth of colour and range of tones, varying from biscuit to a richer tan. It is this stone which gives the house its special character. The east (and principal) front is of the usual 'E' formation, and exhibits those qualities of symmetry and scale so admired by the Elizabethans. Medieval houses were, almost without exception, asymmetrical and low, built higgledy-piggledy round one or more irregular courtyards. In contrast, most Elizabethan houses are almost obsessively symmetrical – front, back and sides – and, as at Montacute, with a matching courtyard with pavilions at the corners. In addition, the average great Elizabethan house is much taller than earlier houses (which seldom exceeded two storeys), and of generally bigger proportions. Montacute is no exception, and the effect of the height of its three storeys is increased by the comparative thinness of the two wings. It is, however, not overwhelming, partly because of the weathered subtleties of the stone used, but also because of two other essentially Elizabethan qualities: the emphasis on fenestration and on architectural detail.

In Gothic architecture the idea had evolved of building churches which resembled lanterns, with great areas of glass and comparatively slight supporting stonework. The Elizabethans applied the same concept to their houses, and in the late sixteenth century it was the height of fashion to have huge areas of glittering glass. Hardwick represents the extreme of this fashion, and Montacute is comparatively restrained. Still, on the east front large windows of three to five lights fill most of the available space with almost continuous bands of glass. The effect, which might otherwise seem hard, is softened by a wealth of architectural detail.

In their approach to such detail the Elizabethans were far more eclectic than their contemporaries in Italy and France, where there was a concerted attempt to re-create the architecture of imperial Rome, both in detail and in principle. The English way was altogether more superficial, and the use of detail decorative rather than organic, to the extent that the Elizabethan Renaissance manner may be seen, not as an innovation, but as a development of the native Gothic tradition. Montacute shows well this architectural equivalent of 'small Latin and less Greek': just enough to suggest that the builder of the house was a man of taste and fashion. The detail of this sort at Montacute is nearly all concentrated on the east front. The three storeys are divided by classical entablatures, some of the windows have pediments, chimneys are shaped like columns, and balustrades abound. Between the windows of the top storey and on the gable of the central bay are

One of the statues of the Nine Worthies that decorate the top storey of the east front

This elaborate carved wooden porch once formed the entrance to the Library; watercolour by C.J. Richardson, 1834

statues of the Nine Worthies (the biblical Joshua, David, and Judas Maccabaeus, the classical Hector, Alexander, and Julius Caesar, and the medieval King Arthur, Charlemagne and Godfrey of Bouillon), awkward but engaging figures, whose classicism goes little further than their Roman dress. Other 'classical' features of the façade include the pairs of shell-headed niches below the ground-floor windows, and the circular niches below the first-floor windows (which may have been intended to contain busts *à l'antique*). All this is topped by curvaceous gables of Flemish type – a fashion imported in the 1570s – superbly decorative, but in no sense classical.

It seems appropriate to call the style theatrical, and this effect of theatre is intensified when we note that, as we proceed round to the back of the house, entablatures become string courses, the columnar chimneys are replaced by square stacks, and some of the gables lose their Flemish accent. Only the semi-circular oriel windows of the Long Gallery, high up on the north and south sides, continue the element of spectacle, and the original west front, also of conventional E-shaped plan, was notably plain. All this underlines the fact that Phelips's house was intended to impress with its initial impact – a powerful piece of self-advertisement. For all that, the exterior has poetry and charm, elements which Arnold must have brought to the design.

If the exterior of Montacute expresses a social purpose, so does the interior, which is in layout quite conventional for the period. The entrance porch gives access to a Screens Passage, dividing the domestic offices on the south side from the Great Hall on the north. This Great Hall, which is divided from the Screens Passage by an elaborate single-storey screen, was the first room of state of the house. Here the servants of the house would have gathered, when not otherwise employed, and here they ate, chatted and played cards and other games. It was a noisy, companionable room, where Sir Edward would have received his guests, and where would have begun the formal procession of food from the kitchen to the Great Chamber (now the Library) on the first floor. This procession was a vital part of Elizabethan entertainment; all present stood as it passed. From the Great Hall the monumental stone staircase leads to the first floor. Up this Sir Edward would have led his guests to the Great Chamber where they would have dined in state. It was remote from the kitchen, but, whatever the consequences for the food, this undoubtedly added to the length and stateliness of the procession bearing the food. After dinner the company would move to the Withdrawing Room (now the Crimson Dressing Room and Crimson Bedroom), while the Great Chamber was prepared for other entertainment – for dancing, or for a masque or play. In Shakespeare's *A Midsummer Night's Dream*, the play-within-a-play, *Pyramus and Thisbe*, is put on 'between our after-supper and bedtime' in the Great Chamber of the Duke of Athens. Beyond the Withdrawing Room was the 'best Chamber', known since 1651 at least as the Hall Chamber, the best bedroom of the house. It is unlikely that Sir Edward Phelips slept here, for it would have been reserved for very grand visitors. The fact that such a large room could be set aside for only occasional use was in itself an index of the owner's wealth.

The decoration and fitting out of these rooms would have been in accord with their importance, and much of this survives. The Great Hall had its elaborate screen, paved floor (now covered), oak panelling, handsome fireplace and a fine show of armorial stained glass, but grandest of all was the Great Chamber, where an especially elaborate fireplace combines with fine panelling, ornate plaster frieze and ceiling, and an especially spectacular display of armorial glass (including the royal arms), to create a *mise-en-scène* of great richness. Here Sir Edward 'kept his state'.

Alongside the conventional sequence of state rooms were many more modest rooms for daily use by Sir Edward, his family and household. The present Parlour on the ground floor was his usual dining-room, while the Drawing Room opposite

was a bedroom. There were more bedrooms (which probably functioned more like modern bed-sitting-rooms) on the first and second floors, these last leading off the Long Gallery. The Long Gallery was the most important room in the house generally reserved for the family, but may also have been used from time to time as an alternative to the Great Chamber. This impressive room extends the full length of the house, and would have been used by the family for recreation, especially in wet weather, the oriels affording fine views of the grounds and surrounding countryside. It is possible that it originally had a tunnel vault ceiling – the present ceiling dates from the time of John Phelips (1784–1834) – with rich plasterwork decoration like those which survive at Chastleton House, Oxfordshire, and Lanhydrock, though the survey of 1667 states simply that it was 'Wainscoted'. Whatever its decoration, by its sheer size and scale it amply proclaimed Sir Edward's importance to all who saw it.

Montacute from the south-east, showing the fine oriel window which terminates the southern end of the Long Gallery

CHAPTER THREE
THE LATER PHELIPS FAMILY

Sir Edward Phelips died in 1614, and was succeeded by his eldest son Sir Robert (1586–1638). As Member of Parliament for East Looe in Cornwall (1604–11), for Saltash in the same county in the 'Addled' Parliament (1614), for Bath (1621) and for Somerset (1624), this able but impetuous man frequently found himself a figure in opposition to the King. A vigorous opponent of corruption in government, he served in 1621 as chairman of the committee of enquiry into the charges of bribery brought against Lord Chancellor Bacon, and in his portrait attributed to Hendrik Gerritsz. Pot painted in 1632, eleven years after the event, he is shown holding in his hand 'Mr. Egertons Petitio[n]'.

Sir Robert Phelips (1586–1638), the son of the builder of Montacute; attributed to Hendrick Gerritsz. Pot (Great Hall)

Egerton was one of the chief witnesses against Bacon, and this allusion stresses the importance of the enquiry to Phelips.

Strongly anti-Catholic, Phelips opposed James I's plans for a marriage between Prince Charles and the Spanish Infanta, and as a result was arrested at Montacute in January 1622 and imprisoned in the Tower of London for eight months. Undaunted, he returned to the Commons and, alongside men such as Pym, Hampden, Strode and Mainwaring, played a leading role in the opposition to the hated royal favourite, the Duke of Buckingham. From that time onwards Phelips's attitude is harder to define, so much so that in 1629 Charles I wrote to him, urging him to look to the interest of the King rather than to 'the favour of the multitude'. However, in 1635 he led the opposition in Somerset to the payment of the hated Ship Money. He died 'of a cold, choked with phlegm' on the eve of the Civil War, convinced of the 'wicked folly' of the course of action which the King was pursuing.

At Montacute Sir Robert had lived in great style. The 1638 Inventory taken at his death lists quantities of expensive and colourful furnishings, and gold and silver plate which alone was valued at £470. Inevitably, such opulence put strains on his finances, and among the first of the creditors to sue was his stepmother. To clear his debts Sir Robert arranged a marriage between his eldest son, Edward, and Ann Pye, whose rich father, Sir Robert Pye of Faringdon, Berkshire, Auditor of the Exchequer, agreed to pay off the creditors on condition that Montacute House was made over forthwith to Edward. This Sir Robert did, though he bequeathed his personal estate, including the contents of the house, to his wife Bridget, to supplement her diminished inheritance, imploring his son to behave in such a way that Lady Phelips did not 'unfurnish the house'.

Life at Montacute in the early years of the Civil

War cannot have been especially congenial. Soon after Sir Robert's death Edward (c.1613–80) justified his father's apprehension by quarrelling with Lady Phelips, who wrote to him on 29 June 1638 in a tone of well-seasoned complaint:

Ned either be licke a sonne, or els hold me as dead, and forgotten, for now I am but mocked with the titel of honered Mother on the outside of a Letter, wch I assure you doth but add affliction to the afflicted.

I wish you serrusly call to mind the promise you made to your deying father, and then if your hart be not turned to stone, you may fear that on daye you shall give a strict account for the breach of it, when honeyed frases in Letters will stand you in no stead, before that just judg who knows the secrets of your hart; Ned doe not for yor owne credit sufer yor ffathers slips to be brought upon the stage, to his dishoner, by your undutyfullness towards me, but consider the oblygation wch leys on you towards him by looking on the fayre and plentyfull estate he hath left you, being neer 100£ a yeare, and how to make you great he hath made some, if not all the rest of his children but a degree better than beggars, for the present, I have no more to say for this tyme, but must rest

Yor unhappey Mother
Bridgett Phellipss

Much of the rest of Edward's life was lived in an atmosphere of impending crisis. Both he and his brother Robert fought for the King in the Civil War, and the story goes that Edward sold the Montacute tapestries to raise funds for the Royalist cause. This may well be true, for many of the textiles recorded in the house in the 1638 Inventory do not feature in later lists, but Edward may simply have been short of money himself. When events began to turn against the King, Edward's loyalty weakened, and, along with many other landowners who were unwilling to risk forfeiture of their estates, in 1646 he quit the Royalist army, and paid the fine of £1,276 imposed on him by Parliament a year later. Robert Phelips, who had less to lose, continued to fight for the King; he was at the Battle of Worcester in 1651, and helped Charles II to escape to France in the aftermath.

Impoverished by the consequences of the war, Colonel Edward was in no position to pay the substantial legacies and annuities left by his father. This provoked family squabbles, some of which

Col. Edward Phelips (c.1613–80), a Royalist officer during the Civil War; attributed to Jacob Huysmans, 1663 (Great Hall)

ripened into court actions. Eventually, in 1651, a commission of sequestration was appointed to raise the £1,202 which was owed, and the long list of items sold from Montacute by the commissioners includes most of the furniture from the state rooms.

After the Restoration in 1660 Colonel Edward was proposed for Charles II's new Order, the Knights of the Royal Oak, with an income of £1,500 per annum, and the King granted him some potentially lucrative offices. He represented Somerset in the Cavalier Parliament, and from 1660 until his death he was Deputy Lieutenant of the county. Despite the outward signs of success, it is clear that he remained in financial difficulties, and in 1668 he made over the Montacute estate to his son and moved out of the great house into Abbey Farmhouse, where he died in 1680.

A country gentleman of traditional leanings and little imagination, Edward Phelips III (1638–99) served in the Somerset militia of horse as lieutenant (by 1661), lieutenant-colonel (1666) and colonel (by 1679–87), and was returned as MP for the family borough of Ilchester, 4 miles from Montacute, at the elections of 1661 and 1685. In the 1690s he represented the county. His portrait shows a man of military aspect, tense and determined, but records show that, in the House of Commons at least, he was less than active. Knighted by Charles II in 1666, he took over the Montacute estate in 1668 and finally succeeded his father in 1680. In the county he was a fierce enemy to his political rivals and an opponent of religious dissent. He was foreman of the grand jury (1680) on the Taunton radicals, and was described two years later as 'very successful in bringing non-conformists to Church'. In the aftermath of the Rye House Plot (1683) he assisted in the search of the houses of 'fanatics' in Bridgwater, and burned the furnishings of their chapel. In 1685 he was ordered to lead his militia against the Duke of Monmouth's invasion, but, in spite, or perhaps because, of the careful training he had given them, they refused to follow him.

More evidence of Sir Edward's shortcomings as a leader emerge after the Glorious Revolution of

Sir Edward Phelips III (1638–99), served as colonel in the Somerset militia of horse; by an unknown artist, 1685 (Great Hall)

1688, when his long-standing political associate Lord Fitzhardinge proposed his reappointment as colonel of the militia. To this the Earl of Shrewsbury objected, noting that 'the county is generally unwilling to serve under [him], remembering the severities used by him towards them, which were different from the carriage of all other who are in command'. He was twice married, and by his second wife, Edith Blake, had three daughters. True to family form, he left a will of such outstanding complexity that it was unclear what passed to his eldest daughter and what to the three sisters in common. Lady Phelips, however, was appointed executrix, with power to manage the property, which she did until her death in 1728.

At the close of the seventeenth century the future of Montacute must have seemed clouded with uncertainties. But from the confusion emerges the figure of Sir Edward's nephew, Edward Phelips IV (1678–1734), the son of his younger brother John, who determined to turn the situation to his advantage. He began by marrying Sir Edward's eldest and favourite daughter, Ann. She, however, died in 1707 after the birth of their second daughter, and he then married her sister, Elizabeth. If this family quadrille seems strange today, it nevertheless had the ultimate effect of securing the family inheritance. Little practical, however, could be done during Lady Phelips's lifetime, and both estate and house fell into a state of neglect. By 1728, the year of Lady Phelips's death, the Great Chamber, once the grandest Day Room in the house, had degenerated into a store for elm boards and 'other Lumber Goods'; earlier in the century Phelips was already bemoaning 'the present mean condition of the place of our Ancestors'.

When, in 1728 Lady Phelips died, Edward and Elizabeth set about reuniting the family possessions. Edward believed that the main estate had been left by old Sir Edward to his eldest daughter Ann (his own first wife), who had bequeathed her interest in it, not to himself, but to their daughters, Anne and Bridget. In 1734, therefore, Edward offered to buy out Anne for £10,000; but he died shortly after, of a 'sweating fever', and it was his widow who 'perfected' the contract, and who made a similar deal with Bridget. The girls did well, very well as it turned

Elizabeth (1689–1750), daughter of Sir Edward Phelips III, with her son Edward (1725–97); by an unknown artist, 1731 (Screens Passage). She married her cousin, Edward Phelips IV (1678–1734), and their son continued the Phelips line at Montacute

Edward Phelips V (1725–97), who rebuilt the west front of Montacute with carved stonework from Clifton Maybank; by an unknown artist, 1765 (Great Hall)

out, because the lawyers shortly after decided that old Sir Edward had really intended to divide the estate among his *three* daughters, and not give it all to his eldest. Thus Elizabeth was entitled to a third share in her own right, and had purchased only a third share from her step-daughters for the price of a half. She went on to tackle her younger sister Edith, wife of Carew Mildmay, who, as she had no surviving children, seems to have relinquished her share quite willingly. (This exceedingly complex arrangement will be better understood if the family tree is studied.)

During the long minority of her only son Edward (he was only nine years of age when his father died), Elizabeth managed the estate. She emerges from her surviving letters as conscientious and firm, but not without a sense of humour. In her correspondence with the family lawyer she is most business-like, and in clipped sentences asks for tenancy reviews and the diligent pursuit of debtors, while her early letters to the family reveal a

vivacious interest in London fashions and the latest gossip. At her death in 1750 the bulk of the family estates was reunited in the hands of her son Edward.

A kindly young man, with a genuine concern for the well-being of his family and the inhabitants of Montacute, Edward Phelips V (1725–97) trained as a lawyer in London. His manuscript diary and autobiography suggest, however, that his happiest moments were spent in the country, in the company of friends who shared his passion for hunting. In 1774, at the age of 49, he became the fifth member of his family to represent the county of Somerset in Parliament. He was perhaps prompted more by family tradition than personal ambition, and the *Public Ledger* notes in 1779 that he 'votes constantly with the ministry, and seems much fitter for parish or turnpike business, than to be the representative of a great county in Parliament'. He apparently never made a speech in the House, though he did witness one notable event:

1778, 7 April, the Great Earl Chatham fell Down as he was speaking in the house of Lords. I was very near him and much affected, he never perfectly recovered .

At the election of 1780 there was trouble over Phelips's nomination, and he resigned the seat 'to preserve the Peace of the County and my own hard acquired Private family Fortune and Estate Unimpared'.

When Phelips came into the estate at the death of his mother, it was 'incumbered with a Debt of Twenty Two Thousand Pounds', and he was forced to sell some land immediately. However, he soon brought a prosperity to Montacute unknown since the time of the first Sir Edward. In this he was helped by two inheritances: in 1765, when his step-sister's husband, Sir Gerrard Napier, bequeathed him substantial properties in the county, and in 1772, when he became the sole heir of his aunt Edith. These windfalls allowed him to make several improvements to Montacute.

Edward's diary for 1778 describes work in the Hall and 'Drawing Room'. Earlier works may well

(Opposite page) The Clifton Maybank frontispiece was added to the west front by Edward Phelips in the 1780s

have gone unrecorded: the folly on St Michael's Hill, for example, bears the date 1760. Fortunately, the construction of the new west front to the house is well documented.

Until the late eighteenth century the main approach to the house led to the east front. In 1785, however, Edward decided to make a new drive:

On the 19th of December I began Forming a New Road to the West Front of Montacute house from the publick Road thro Boys Court Orchard by Filling Up Millponds Levelling Hedges etc: And in the Course of the Xmas Hollidays I began Digging the foundation for the New West Front which were very great and Arduous Undertakings at My advanced season of Life.

The serpentine drive was completed by the end of January 1786: from the main road it curved gently south before heading east to the house. Hand in hand with this change of axis went the creation of the new west front, erected between the existing projecting wings, across the recessed central block. A glance at the plans (p. 50) reveals how this change had the effect of forming at ground- and first-floor levels a corridor linking the projecting wings, and giving on the first floor independent access to each bedroom, where previously they had been inter-linked – a significant modernisation indicative of the growing demand for privacy.

The new front was built of Ham stone, and it harmonises well with the Elizabethan house without losing its identity; slotted in between the three-storey wings, it creates a sequence of advancing and retiring wall surfaces, often dramatised by the afternoon sun. Its most remarkable feature, however, is the carved ornament, which, as Edward explains in his autobiography under 1786, came from Clifton Maybank, a house near Yeovil, built by Sir John Horsey, c.1546–64:

On the second of May My Wife & Self attended the Sale of the Materials of Clifton House then Pulling Down we bought . . . The Porch, Arms, Pillars and all the Ornamental Stone of the Front to be Transferred to the Intended West Front of Montacute.

Edward used the Clifton Maybank carvings to crown his new work, deploying the fluted shafts to animate the walls and crowding the parapet with heraldic beasts. The magnificent relief above the entrance came from the porch at Clifton Maybank; at its centre Edward substituted his own coat of arms for that of the Horseys. This heraldic achievement is supported by two *putti*, with above them horses' heads, in punning reference to the name of Horsey (the horse motif is also found on the tomb of Sir John Horsey and his father in Sherborne Abbey, which incorporates a heraldic panel very similar to the one at Montacute, although of cruder work-manship). Altogether the carvings show an eclectic blend of Gothic and Renaissance motifs – the late Gothic band of quatrefoils and shields above the heraldic panel, for instance, is joined with Renais-sance *putti* – and, though a similar mixture of styles is found elsewhere in England in the mid-sixteenth century, the quality of the Clifton carvings is so exceptional that it has been attributed to French masons. Certainly this hybrid style flourished in France in the early sixteenth century. To gauge their quality it is worth comparing the athletic Clifton Maybank *putti* with the Elizabethan Worthies on the east front, whose Roman armour cannot dis-guise their strange proportions and sturdy but inexpressive limbs, surely the work of local masons.

The west front has been compared with examples of 'Elizabethan Revival' architecture, such as 'Capability' Brown's additions to Corsham Court in Wiltshire and the summer-house at Burghley House in Northamptonshire, both built in the 1760s. However, Phelips is silent about his reasons for wishing to remodel the west front, and this should warn against any attempt to class him with the amateur exponents of Rococo taste such as Horace Walpole. It is nevertheless interesting to speculate why the façade was *not* classical, at a time when this was the prevalent style. Perhaps it was an inherent sense of decorum which persuaded him not to graft a classical addition on a Tudor stock, but opportunism and family piety may also have played a part: the stonework from Clifton Maybank was available, and in the carved panel now above the west porch of Montacute, alongside the monogram of Sir John Horsey, builder of Clifton Maybank, is that of his wife Edith Phelips, aunt of the builder of Montacute. Whatever the immediate stimulus, by 1787 Montacute had a new carriage drive and a new façade, befitting the dignity of an important local landowner and former MP, whose eldest son had represented the county in his turn since 1784. The new corridor behind the Clifton Maybank façade was not finally opened up until February 1788.

Edward Phelips was succeeded in 1797, not by his eldest son, Edward VI, who predeceased him in 1791, but by his second son William (1755–1806), Vicar of Yeovil. (The brothers were both painted by the Bath artist Thomas Beach.) At this time the family had a distinctly clerical cast: William's younger brother Charles had been ordained; William's wife was the daughter of the Vicar of Doulting, Somerset; three of their seven sons took holy orders; and one of their four daughters married a parson.

William's eldest son, John (1784–1834), escaped the clerical vocation, but was nevertheless noted for his kindly and charitable disposition. It was, for instance, his habit to walk the Borough – the village square – and if he found anyone out of a job, he would give them work on the estate; on one occasion he hired some unemployed quarrymen to fill up the lake in the park, seen in the engraving published in Collinson's *History of Somerset*. As

John Phelips (1784–1834); by an unknown artist, c.1820–5 (Great Hall)

Chairman of the Somerset Quarter Sessions he had the reputation of 'a prompt and efficient dispenser of justice'.

In 1828 J. P. Neale wrote in his *Views of the Seats of Noblemen* that Phelips 'had spared no expense' in restoring the house, but no documentary evidence of his work survives. There is, though, a tradition that he redecorated the Long Gallery with disastrous consequences, for, in heightening the ceiling, the cross-beams were severed, seriously weakening the roof structure. It may therefore be significant that Neale described the gallery in the past tense, and that no furniture is recorded there in the two inventories taken after John Phelips's death in 1834. One, a list of heirlooms to be included in the entailed estate which went to his nephew William, and the other a catalogue of his personal belongings, to be sold for the benefit of his widow. 'The Splendid and Modern Household Goods and Furniture' described in the catalogue comprised 462 lots in the house alone. It is open to conjecture whether the 'modern' furnishings had been purchased by John or his father. Along with quantities of mahogany furniture are a number of items that indicate the way in which the family passed their time: a billiard table and scientific instruments, including a barometer, hydrometer, a theodolite, a pentograph and a telescope. The presence of an 'Elegant piccolo pianoforte', a 'Hand Organ (forty tunes) by Longman', grand pianos, a 'Square Piano-forte, by Broadwood', a 'Double acting pedal harp with gold mountings', and a 'Painted box with musical glasses' suggests that musical evenings were a feature of John Phelips's years at Montacute, and the impression of conviviality is heightened by a 'very extensive and choice stock of the most approved vintages of Portugal, Spain, France, the Rhine, etc. etc.'

John Phelips died in 1834, his wife remarried and moved to Dorset, and Montacute passed to his eleven-year-old nephew William (1823–89). During his minority the house was let to John Serell, but in 1845 William, aged 22, married a rich woman, Ellen Helyar, and took up residence.

Early in their married life the Phelipses travelled in Europe, and Ellen's journals reveal a well-schooled interest in topography and architecture,

William Phelips (1823–89), with Montacute in the background; by T. M. Joy, 1858 (Parlour Passage)

and a critical appreciation of continental food. The couple were particularly fond of Italy, and William's passport records visits to Florence in 1847, 1848 and 1850. During the 1850s they seem to have spent more time at Montacute with their two children, but family life was soon disrupted by the first symptoms of William's mental instability, which apparently reached a crisis in 1860. The exact nature of the illness is not known, but its most obvious manifestation seems to have been compulsive gambling. Llewelyn Powys, whose father was vicar of Montacute in the 1880s, records in his *Somerset Essays* (1937) that the squire had

inherited eighteenth-century tastes, and through his love of gaming had so compromised the Phelips estate that it never afterwards recovered. In the hall [at Montacute] there is an oil painting of him standing life-size in his park, tall hat in hand, the great house he ruined reduced by perspective to the size of a doll's house.

Near Ilchester there are two farms called Sock and Beerly . . . I was told by the country people this story about them. The Gambling Squire was staying at

Weymouth, and on a wet afternoon, having nothing to do, staked a bet on one of two flies that were crawling up the window-pane. When his friend's fly reached the wooden plinth which marked the winning post of this fantastic race, the idle sparks who were watching heard the Master of Montacute mysteriously exclaim, 'There go Sock and Beerly!'

Of Ellen Phelips, the daughter of the poet Shelley's first cousin and first love, Powys writes:

I do not think I have ever seen an old lady with so delicate a complexion. Even in her great age the poise of her head was light and graceful as a rose upon its stalk. The moulding of her skull was as fragile as that of the most precious porcelain and there was a flush upon her cheeks that reminded me of the inside of some of the sea shells in my father's cabinet.

In the early years of their marriage this oddly assorted couple did much to improve Montacute and its grounds. In his *Baronial Halls* (1848), S. C. Hall described Montacute during William's minority as 'stripped in great degree of its internal decorations', and so little is known about Uncle John's 'restorations' that it is impossible to assess the state of the house when William took up residence in 1845. However, a small collection of architectural drawings survives which suggests that they had ambitious plans for improvements. The drawings are neither signed nor dated, but their style suggests they are probably by Louis Vulliamy (1791–1871), a prolific architect whose work for the wealthy landowner R. S. Holford included Dorchester House, an opulent *palazzo* in London's Park Lane, and Westonbirt, a festive 'Elizabethan' pile in Gloucestershire. The Montacute drawings show a new service court built on to the south side of the house, with a bakery, brew-house, dairy, vast servants' hall and ample brushing and boot rooms. There were also to be ancillary offices such as larders, a 'place for vegetables' and a scullery leading off the kitchen (which remained in the main house). Perhaps because of lack of funds this new range was never built. Instead, William remodelled the existing service court, which survives today as the Trust's tea-room and shop. In her diary for 1853 William's mother-in-law, Mrs Helyar, noted 'the alterations in their yard which is much improved by lowering the old buildings'. Aesthetically this was a wise decision, in contrast to Vulliamy's scheme, in which it was planned to deck his new range with obelisks, balustrading and banded pilasters, all competing for attention with the main house.

Internally, it was proposed to extend the Library the whole length of the north wing, with new bay windows overlooking the north garden and an 'Elizabethan' plasterwork ceiling. Similar ceilings were planned for the Hall, Parlour and Drawing Room. These ambitious projects lapsed, but certain features in the house are recorded in the drawings, notably the north entrance, the Long Gallery ceiling (with minor variations), and the Library ceiling. The majority of the bedrooms were probably renovated at this time, and some retain fragments of Elizabethan Revival panelling and plasterwork, no

doubt survivors of this modernisation. Work began soon after 1845 and was finished by 1852, when Mrs Helyar showed friends round the house.

Unfortunately there is very little evidence of how William and Ellen re-equipped the house, for their furniture has long since vanished. A photograph of the Library taken about 1890, however, shows vestiges of Elizabethan Revival furnishings: bookcases adorned with strapwork and barley-sugar columns, and a set of chairs and pelmets *en suite*, the latter hung with lambrequin valances. All that remains today are the bookcases, stripped of their fancy dress, and the ceiling. Ironically, the style survives better out of doors: it is apparent in the stable block, built after 1860, on the site of the

Ellen Phelips with her granddaughter and historian of the Phelips family, Marjorie Ingilby, and her great-granddaughter, Cecily, c.1906

Montacute became a popular source of inspiration for Elizabethan Revival architects in the early nineteenth century. Joseph Nash's 'Mansions of England' (1841) illustrates the Clifton Maybank frontispiece

previous stables, and manifest in the South Lodge. It is also discernible in the layout of the grounds.

When Edward Phelips rebuilt the west front in 1786, his antiquarian taste was in advance of the time. Renovating the house some sixty years later, William Phelips would have had no difficulty persuading his architect about the aesthetic merits of Montacute, for the Elizabethan Revival was in full swing. In 1835 a parliamentary select committee recommended that the new Palace of Westminster be in the Gothic or Elizabethan style.

In the early nineteenth century, pioneers of the style visited Montacute: John Buckler and his son John Chessell first went there about 1811. J. P. Neale described the house in *Views of the Seats of Noblemen* (second series, volume IV, 1828). C. J. Richardson

made a series of drawings and watercolours of the house between 1834 and 1841, some of which were published in his own *Studies From Old English Mansions* (1841–5) and in S. C. Hall's *The Baronial Halls* (1848). Joseph Nash included a view of the west porch in *The Mansions of England* (third series, 1841). With these books the architectural and decorative features of Montacute entered the vocabulary of the Elizabethan Revival, frequently quoted, and as frequently misquoted by Victorian architects. Of the houses contemporary with Montacute, perhaps Charlecote Park is the most complete surviving example of a wholesale revivalist renovation.

During William Phelips's years of mental illness, the estate was run by his younger brother, Captain Richard Phelips, who supervised the rebuilding of the old coachhouse and stables, which had fallen into a dilapidated and dangerous condition. He also headed the building committee which restored the parish church and contributed handsomely to the cost of the work.

In 1875 William Phelips's son William Robert (1846–1919) married and assumed responsibility for the house, which then entered its final phase of occupation by the Phelips family. As a young man the eccentric Phelips astonished the inhabitants of Montacute with a lecture in the Montacute National School Room on 'The Nature and effects of Combustion', in the course of which he demonstrated the mysteries of 'Fire in Water' and 'Pharaoh's Serpents'. Later he introduced the benefits of 'fire in water' to Montacute, when in 1876 the firm of G. N. Haden & Son of Trowbridge was consulted about a central heating system. However, he could only afford to install hot pipes on the ground floor and just one bath. As the niece of William Robert's wife, Cicely, wrote, 'The Phelipses were not at this period a wealthy family and no great state was kept up . . . The house being of such vast proportions a practically separate establishment could be arranged, but this naturally meant alterations. The great chamber was made into a library and sitting-room for the old lady and her daughter [William Robert's mother and sister]. It had its own lobby and Mrs Phelips' bedroom was the celebrated garden room which opens out of it. It was at this time that the inner porch was removed from the council chamber (now once more restored) and made into a wardrobe for my aunt's clothes, and placed in her bedroom.' William Robert also encouraged a number of improvements to the village, laying mains water, sewerage and gas pipes, and offering land for a railway station and new housing. The family's financial difficulties increased until the estate and William Robert were virtually insolvent. During his father's illness, properties had been let on long leases or otherwise neglected; rents had remained low, and there had been no capital investment. As a result, William Robert did not have the means to live at Montacute. By selling the family silver and pictures (apart from the portraits) in 1895 he delayed his departure by a few years, but in 1911 he arranged a lease of the house to Robert Davidson for £650 per annum, and the estate was slowly dismembered, beginning with the disposal of outlying farms, and culminating in the sale of most of Abbey Farm in 1918. When Phelips died in the following year, Lord Curzon was the tenant of Montacute. Powys comments in appropriately melancholy moralising vein on this decline:

I do not think any occurrence I have observed in my life has given me sharper understanding of the insubstantiality of all temporal values than the separation of this house from the Phelipses.

William Robert Phelips (1846–1919) having his portrait painted in the Library, 1897

CHAPTER FOUR

THE REVIVAL OF MONTACUTE

In 1915 the estate agents Knight, Frank & Rutley negotiated the lease of Montacute for that 'most superior person' George Nathaniel Curzon, Earl (and later Marquess) Curzon, at the time Lord Privy Seal in Asquith's Coalition Cabinet. With characteristic attention to a bargain, Curzon stressed the decayed condition of the house, and succeeded in reducing the rent to £550 per annum, though he agreed to install electric light and redecorate the house at his own cost. This last task he entrusted to his mistress, the prolific authoress Elinor Glyn. In 1907 her novel, *Three Weeks*, was judged scandalous by many who had not read it, and achieved for her a notoriety which was intensified by her passionate nature, evident eccentricities, and fondness for exotic furs, commemorated in the clerihew:

> Would you like to sin
> with Elinor Glyn
> on a tiger skin?
> Or would you prefer
> to err
> with her
> on some other fur?

She was devoted to Curzon, and spent much of the autumn and winter of 1915 and of the following year working at the house. This is all the more remarkable, for she had notably sybaritic tastes, and could not normally abide room temperatures below 70°F. At Montacute she endured arctic conditions in the name of love, and spent much of her time up step-ladders in huge unheated rooms. Unfortunately neither correspondence nor accounts relating to the work have come to light, and hardly anything of her schemes for the rooms survives. In any case, her enjoyment of Montacute was short-lived; she sensed Curzon's feelings cooling, but it nevertheless came as a devastating shock to her when she read in *The Times* on 11 December 1916 the notice of his engagement to Mrs Alfred Dug-

gan. There was no word of explanation; she never saw or wrote to him again, and she burnt nearly five hundred of his letters, some of which no doubt told of their schemes for Montacute.

From the start Curzon was a difficult tenant, and as early as June 1915 complained that 'there is no service of glass . . . the dinner service is unfit for use . . . the cooking utensils unfit . . . blankets missing . . .', and – the final impertinence – no scuttles. It is evident that Curzon did not take on Montacute for convenience's sake and spent little time in residence there. He had a genuine love of old buildings, and spent much of his life and fortune restoring them: in addition to Montacute, there was the family home, Kedleston, in Derbyshire, Tattershall Castle in

The novelist Elinor Glyn lived briefly at Montacute with Lord Curzon and helped him to redecorate the house

Lincolnshire and Bodiam Castle in East Sussex.
The

writ

Con
reca
histo
the
it w
the
hav
histo

It
cute
ind
vita
nin
his
was
the
bal
he
hou
ten

E
bitt
bac
zor
am
at l
had
the
Cu
wa
abi
his
pu
Pri
sen
ho
wa
tel
wh
tra
me
ov

aft

... Montacute from 1915 until his death in ... the bath concealed within a Jacobean- ... e room that now bears his name

surviving son of William Robert,
...ving in Canada since 1913, felt he
...e but to sell the house which his
...rother, Edward (d.1928), had been
...ispose of for several years. The
...eady been removed in an abortive
...e house to Lord Waring, of Waring
...avish sale brochures expatiated on
... architectural importance of 'the
...Montacute House'. The house was
...moderate size only and compara-
...e to maintain': it had twenty-five
...essing-rooms, six baths, and addi-
...dation for menservants. With it
...e hundred acres of land, including
...and twelve 'Old World Cottages'.
...the mansion included an 'Eton
... of £8, and the owners were 'liable
... the Chancel of the Parish Church'.
...onsolation that 'many well known
...re in easy reach'.

...gered on the market for two years,
...e Marjorie Ingilby (1877–1957),
...illiam Robert Phelips, began to
...through the large accumulation of
...ow in the Somerset Record Office),

31

Ernest Cook helped to rescue Montacute by buying the house and presenting it through the Society for the Preservation of Ancient Buildings to the National Trust in 1931

laying the foundation of all subsequent research on the family. By 1931 Montacute was valued at £5,882 'for scrap' and its future looked bleak. Rescue was, however, at hand in the person of Ernest Cook, grandson of Thomas Cook, founder of the travel agency of that name, a bachelor and naturally reclusive (though he had run the firm's banking department). In 1930 the Cook family sold the firm to the Wagons Lits company of France, and Ernest devoted his life to good works. A year later he offered a large sum of money to the Society for the Preservation (now Protection) of Ancient Buildings for the purchase of suitable properties. A. R. Powys, the Society's Secretary (and brother of Llewelyn Powys who wrote so evocatively about Montacute), son of a former vicar of Montacute and a childhood friend of the Phelips family, took Cook

to Montacute. He agreed to purchase the house for presentation to the National Trust, as the SPAB was not empowered to hold property. However, no money was found to buy any of the contents offered by Lady Curzon, and when Montacute opened in 1932, it was virtually bare, save for the Phelips family portraits and Lord Curzon's bath. It was also tenantless, and, more crucially, had no endowment. To James Lees-Milne it seemed by the mid-1930s to be 'an empty and rather embarrassing white elephant'.

During the Second World War Montacute was used as one of the stores of the Victoria and Albert Museum, and was looked after by the Ministry of Works, but, as early as 1944 – before the Trust regained possession of the house – Eardley Knollys, agent for the Trust's Southern Region, decided that it was essential to attempt to furnish it if it were to be opened to the public after the war. In 1945 he persuaded Lord Zetland, Chairman of the Trust, to write to *The Times* appealing for suitable pieces, and, shortly after, a committee, chaired by Sir Geoffrey Hippisley Cox, was set up to bring the scheme to completion. Over the next two years Knollys and Lees-Milne set to work arranging the contents. They had money only for a little distemper, and nothing for the curtains, carpets, china, books and furniture which were needed to turn the empty shell into a furnished house. Working informally, with a minimum of bureaucracy, little time and no money, Silk Purses Ltd (as they called themselves) got the house ready to open in July 1946. Vita Sackville-West, a friend of both men, came down to advise on the gardens, and ended up planting them herself with the assistance of Knollys.

In 1951 the industrialist Sir Malcolm Stewart (1872–1951), a friend of Hippisley Cox, bequeathed his collection of tapestries, pictures, furniture and early works of art to the Trust for

the adornment of Montacute House in order that it may re-assume its former character as the stately home of an English gentleman as distinct from the aspect of a museum.

These finally came to the house after the death of Lady Stewart in 1960, and, though some of the objects are somewhat grander than anything the Phelips family ever owned, they undoubtedly add an exceptional lustre to the other more modest gifts and loans which had accumulated at Montacute since 1946.

The advent of the Stewart bequest underlined the need to take in hand the decoration of the house, with the aim of uniting house and contents as a whole. A start was made with the Drawing Room, which was hung with the present flock wallpaper, and the chimney-piece from Coleshill in Berkshire installed, a sad reminder of Ernest Cook's greatest gift to the Trust, destroyed by fire in 1952. But Montacute had to wait until 1972–4 for further redecoration, when the National Portrait Gallery became involved.

Throughout the 1960s it had become increasingly obvious that Montacute, without endowment, was in difficulties. It was failing to attract the numbers of visitors needed, and this against a background of rising overheads. The decision to approach the National Portrait Gallery for help with the empty Long Gallery – a spectacular room, but one which seemed to lack a *raison d'être* – was the inspiration of the late Lord Rosse, then Chairman of the Trust's Properties Committee. He discussed the National Portrait Gallery's plans for decentralisation with its

Director, Roy Strong, and the Gallery and the Trust seized on the idea of a joint venture. The result was a display of nearly a hundred sixteenth- and seventeenth-century portraits of historic interest from the Gallery's collections (see Chapter Five). Together they worked with John Fowler, the Trust's adviser on decoration, on renovating and redecorating the Long Gallery and adjoining rooms, and the exhibition opened to the public in 1975. Montacute has come to life and the outpost of the Gallery is an undoubted success, as is shown by the increasing numbers of visitors who come to the house each year, bringing a much needed supplement to the Trust's income. Nevertheless, it is unlikely that Montacute will ever be self-supporting, and the programme of works which continues is carried out in an atmosphere of financial uncertainty. In 1980 the Trust initiated a programme of repairs to the stonework of the house, and, with the aid of a substantial grant from the Historic Buildings Council, undertook the reconstruction of the roofs of the two garden pavilions. Much remains to be done, and the raising of large sums of money from public and private sources remains a necessity in the sixtieth year of the Trust's custodianship of this fine house.

In 1929 Montacute was put up for sale

By direction of G. A. PHELIPS, Esq.

Circa 1580.

The Entrance Front.

NOTE.
Montacute House may be viewed only by special appointment through the Auctioneers.

THE WORLD FAMOUS
"MONTACUTE HOUSE"
SOMERSET.

For Sale by Auction (unless previously Sold Privately), at the London Auction Mart, 155, Queen Victoria Street, E.C.
On WEDNESDAY, 3rd JULY, 1929, at 2·30 p.m.

Auctioneers:		Solicitors:
Messrs. JOHN D. WOOD & Co., 6, Mount Street, London, W.I.	acting in conjunction	Messrs. KNIGHT, FRANK & RUTLEY, 20, Hanover Square, London, W.I.	Messrs. HUGH R. POOLE & SON, Under Sheriff's Office, South Petherton, Somerset.

CHAPTER FIVE
TUDOR AND JACOBEAN PORTRAITURE

The careers of artists as far apart in time as Holbein, Lely and Sargent testify to the Englishman's appetite for portraits – of himself, his wife, his children, his friends and associates, and of his sovereign – at the expense of all other kinds of painting. Only likenesses of his house, his horse and his dogs evoked anything like the same enthusiasm.

Nevertheless, before the accession of Henry VIII it was rare indeed for a monarch or any of his subjects to sit for their portrait, and our knowledge of the appearance of the kings and queens and other great figures of the Middle Ages derives largely from written accounts or from the comparatively stylised likeness to be found in illuminated manuscripts, on coins or in tomb sculptures: images which were intended to convey the sitter's rank in the hierarchy of creation, but little of their individuality. Of English kings before Henry VII only Richard II seems certainly to have sat for his portrait, although death masks were generally taken of kings and queens for use in their funeral effigies, and a number of these survive at Westminster Abbey.

The sixteenth century was the first age of portraiture in England, when the establishment of the Tudor dynasty brought prosperity and stability after long years of war. On the Continent, in Italy and in northern Europe as well, the Renaissance had brought with it an awakening interest in men as individuals, and consequently in portraiture, more than a century earlier. Only a very few British merchants and soldiers of fortune were lucky enough to be painted on their travels by the great European artists, as, for instance, Edward Grimston by Petrus Christus (1446). England had no Van Eyck or Memlinc, no Fouquet, no Pisanello for medals, never mind the astonishing profusion of portrait painters of the Italian schools. The consequent scarcity of portraits was to cause a problem in the sixteenth century, when growing national pride and the development of antiquarianism created a demand for likenesses of monarchs and other worthies of the Middle Ages to decorate the Long Galleries and rooms of state of the great houses. Such portraits were often formed into sets, and we know that such sets could be purchased in their entirety from a painter's workshop. The sixteenth-century Hornby Castle set of portraits of the Kings and Queens of England now at Montacute (48–55, 65–72), and formerly in the collection of the Dukes of Leeds, is one of the largest to survive, though it is evident from the style of the portraits that they do not all come from the same workshop. The likenesses of the earliest kings are entirely fictitious. The remainder, from Edward III onwards, are usually related to some painting or effigy with a claim, however dubious, to authenticity. Notable exceptions are the portrait of *Henry IV* (65), based on a print of Charles VI of France, and *Edward V* (67), which seems to derive from the usual portrait-type of Edward VI. Such substitutions were often made when no authentic likeness could be found. Essentially crude as works of art, these portraits with their bold forms, bright colours and lavish use of gold leaf made an impressive show when displayed *en masse* in a Long Gallery.

Though the Renaissance arrived late in England, it brought with it one of its greatest painters, Hans Holbein the Younger (1497/8–1543), who came to London in 1526 with a letter of introduction from the great humanist Erasmus to Sir Thomas More. His portrait of More, of which there is an excellent sixteenth-century version at Montacute (5), demonstrates those qualities of realism, refinement of characterisation and sheer technical accomplishment, which led Henry VIII and his court to patronise him so extensively in the 1530s and '40s. During his period of royal service, Holbein's style became gradually more linear and hieratic, more concerned with surface pattern, as may be seen in the copies of his *Sir William Butts* (7) and *Edward VI* (4). This is perhaps partly because he worked up his painted portraits from drawings made from the life – a useful technique when dealing with busy and demanding courtiers – and perhaps also reflects the influence of the Mannerist movement in international court portraiture. It is this decorative style of Holbein's last years which was taken up by his followers in England, as, for instance, in the late 'Castle Howard' portrait of the King (6), and which remained, in exaggerated form, an influence on Elizabethan portraiture until the end of the century.

Henry's son Edward VI employed the international Mannerist William Scrots, or Stretes (fl. 1537–53), as his court painter, while his eldest daughter Mary I favoured the Fleming Hans Eworth (fl. 1540–73), in whose portraits Holbein's love of line and detail is combined with a delicacy which is the hallmark of the Flemish court style. Eworth's rendering of Mary's rather plain features

(5) Sir Thomas More; after Holbein, 1527

does not seem to have worried her, though it is hard to believe that her half-sister Elizabeth I would have approved so dispassionate a view of her own face. Not surprisingly, therefore, Eworth fell from favour and fashion at Elizabeth's succession, though one or two of his modestly talented compatriots – notably Steven van der Meulen (fl. 1543–68) and Arnold van Brounckhorst (fl. 1566–80) – established substantial portrait practices at court and among the upper ranks of society. Van der Meulen's *Thomas Wentworth, 2nd Baron Wentworth* (12) illustrates the characteristics and limitations of much of the Flemish portraiture of this period: a three-quarter-length showing both hands, the body turned slightly to the left; there is a hint of an architectural background, a glimpse of an ornamental sword hilt, carefully observed but not over elaborate costume, and sturdy, somewhat stolid characterisation and stiff bodily articulation.

Most subsequent Elizabethan portraiture seems to have developed under the influence of the opinions of the Queen herself and of her brilliant miniature painter, Nicholas Hilliard (*c.*1547–1619). In a celebrated passage in his treatise on miniature-painting, *The Arte of Limning*, Hilliard describes the Queen's first sitting to him, about 1572, noting that she

chose her place to sit for that purpose the open alley of a goodly garden where no tree was near, nor any shadow at all.

The crucial phrase is 'nor any shadow at all', for Elizabeth's preference had the effect of banishing from court the shadowed style of the Flemish emigré artists, who worked in the tradition of Renaissance realism. In its place there was established a new court style of portrait-painting: two-dimensional, archaising, with a love of colour, pattern and detail at the expense of characterisation. Although Holbein loved pattern and detail, he also delighted in delineating the movement of light over the surface of a face, the revelation of form, texture and character. In high Elizabethan portraiture, in contrast, the faces are generally reduced to an impassive mask, and painted with the absolute economy of just a few lines. This was a style calculated to please the Queen, who was extremely sensitive about her appearance. In 1563, ten years before she sat to Hilliard, she had already issued a decree forbidding the production of debased images of herself; she intended to sit to an artist and establish an authentic pattern or image of herself which could be copied; a similar proclamation was again issued in 1596.

Although Hilliard is known to have painted the Queen on the scale of life, the responsibility for living up to her ideal in large-scale portraits generally fell to the official court painters – the Serjeant Painters – such as George Gower (c.1540?–96). It is probably Gower's face-pattern of Elizabeth which was used in the 'Armada' portrait (22), and which was reused over and over again in portraits of the Queen by artists of all abilities; only the costume, jewellery and background changes; the mask of the Queen is constant. Given that the face is so stylised and devoid of character, it is easy to see why the emphasis in such a portrait falls on costume and accessories; even her hair is reduced to a repeating pattern of curlicues.

Great Elizabethan houses like Hardwick Hall and Montacute were created for display, both externally and internally, and few houses would have been complete without a show of portraits. The large numbers of surviving portraits from this period testify to this demand, as does the indifferent quality of many of them. There was a huge production of images of the Queen and of her ministers, such as Lord Burghley, which, as the images are copied and recopied, show an increasing degree of stylisation. In the case of the Queen only the costumes vary, and these become more and more splendid as her likeness is reduced to a lifeless icon (36).

Individual portraits of members of her court painted from the life, though they partake of the same style, have an individuality and charm which, though they achieve little or no psychological insight, is irrepressible. George Gower's portrait of *Elizabeth Knollys, Lady Layton* (Dining Room), one of the Queen's maids of honour, painted in 1577, exemplifies this. The doll-like face with bulbous staring eyes (Gower's trademark) is framed by an extravaganza of lace, embroidery and jewels; add to this the coat of arms, crest, motto and inscriptions, all carefully placed about the picture space, and you have a decorative ensemble which is entirely ex-

(36) Elizabeth I; by an unknown artist, c.1585–90

quisite. One detail which catches the eye is the jewel in Lady Layton's hat, made in the form of a starfish surrounded by corals: a natural curiosity is recreated with the greatest artifice, and this costly object epitomises all the extravagance, preciosity and exoticism which characterises Elizabethan taste.

Alongside this preciosity is a tendency to symbolism and allegory of a moralising kind. Sometimes this simply takes the form of a family or personal motto, as in the 1572 portrait of the *1st Earl of Essex* (18) inscribed INVIDIA COMES VIRTUTIS ('envy is the companion of virtue'), but may sometimes be accompanied by a symbolic device or *impresa*, a type of puzzle which the Elizabethans loved. This is the case with the portrait of Sir Philip Sidney's brother, *Robert Sidney, 1st Earl of Leicester* (15), where the Latin motto INVENIAM VIAM AUT FACIAM ('I shall find a way or I shall make one') is linked with a device of boughs bursting into flame. The motto is taken from a French token of 1562, and the device from one of Piero de' Medici's published in Simeoni's *Dialogo dell'Imprese*. This note of learned allusion is intensified in the portrait by a reading of the decoration of Leicester's Milanese shield, which shows Apollo as God of Light and Fire and as God of Fertility, as described in Vincenzo Cartari's *Le Imagini dei Dei degli Antiche*, one of the most widely used of Renaissance mythological manuals.

Some portraits are conceived wholly in allegorical terms, as, for instance, the portraits of *Sir Thomas Chaloner the Elder* (31), *Sir Thomas Coningsby* (33) and *Sir Edward Hoby* (80). The *Chaloner*, though the allegory is given a personal and learned cast, illustrates the conventional moral that all earthly things perish. This is one of the most common themes of portrait mottoes of the period, and it is undoubtedly the case that portraits (so often inscribed with the age of the sitter and date) were viewed as mirrors in which the sitter could see and meditate on the effects of time. The *Coningsby*, probably by Gower and painted in 1572, is equally conventional. In it an allegory of falconry is used to contrast the states of youth and maturity. The *Hoby* of 1583 is both more complex and personal. The young soldier, who was later to catch the eye of James I, is portrayed wearing Greenwich armour, and holding a baton with the motto VANA SINE VIRIBUS IRA ('anger without strength is vain'). In the top right-hand corner, balancing a display of Hoby's arms, top left, is an inset allegorical scene of a woman (perhaps Elizabeth I) coming out of a castle. She holds a scroll inscribed in Latin with a legend signifying 'laid aside but not blunted', and in front of her is a pile of discarded weapons and military trophies with a veil over them. The portrait was painted a year after Hoby's marriage and knighthood, but the exact significance of the allegory, which evidently refers to some temporary interruption of his military service, is not known.

Such allegories are comparatively abstruse. However, many portraits of the Elizabethan period and later were painted to commemorate an event or convey a simple message of some sort, usually about the status of the sitter. No military commander is portrayed without his baton, no officer of the royal household without his white wand, no Knight of the Garter without his insignia. The rich display their wealth, the pious their piety, and widows commemorate their widowhood with a lavish display of weeds and sometimes an urn. Such tendencies continue well into the seventeenth cen-

(33) Sir Thomas Coningsby; attributed to George Gower, 1572

tury (until Van Dyck and Lely largely banished such specific temporal references). *Sir John Backhouse*, painted by the mysterious monogrammist V.M. in 1637 (64), is shown as a bluff city entrepreneur holding a painting of his own greatest speculative achievement, the New River in London. His motto MELIORA SPERO ('I hope for better things') adds a whiff of conventional piety to an otherwise worldly portrait with its thoughts of (presumably) heavenly rather than earthly rewards.

Towards the end of the sixteenth century much of the literature, music and painting is suffused with a tone of melancholy romanticism. It is found in the miniatures of Hilliard, but above all in the work of his fellow miniaturist Isaac Oliver and in that of the dominant portraitist on the scale of life, the Fleming Marcus Gheeraerts the Younger (1561/2–1636), who arrived in London with his father in 1567/8. His *Lady Scudamore* of 1615 (91), with its touching motto 'No Spring till now', surrounded by a garland of flowers, commemorates the marriage of her son, evidently a bright spot in an otherwise melancholy life, and the mood of the portrait catches this note of sunshine amid showers. Gheeraerts's so-called 'Ditchley' portrait of Elizabeth, painted *c.*1592, now in the National Portrait Gallery in London, shows the Queen in all her splendour, but also as an old woman, something which would have hitherto been unthinkable. It also illustrates those elements of fantasy and realism which Gheeraerts blends in his finest portraits. This portrait was painted for Sir Henry Lee of Ditchley

in Oxfordshire, one of the artist's most important patrons and the Queen's champion, for whom Gheeraerts also painted the portrait of *Henry, Prince of Wales* (*c.*1603) at Montacute (60). This is also a full-length, in Garter robes, but of more modest pretensions: the puppet-like figure of the Prince is suspended in an unconvincing picture-space, where the sloping floor, the curtains and a glimpse of landscape hint at a third dimension which is never fully realised.

Alongside Gheeraerts a number of other artists produced series of highly decorative full-length

(64) Sir John Backhouse; by the monogrammist V.M., 1637

portraits in fundamentally Elizabethan style well into the seventeenth century. One such is the recently rediscovered William Larkin (d.1619), whose work is so well represented at Ranger's House in Blackheath. Other artists, like the author of the superbly dandified full-length of the *3rd Earl of Southampton* (46) or the rather less stylish *4th Earl of Pembroke* (58), in Garter robes in the Long Gallery, remain to be identified. Such full-lengths were the equivalent of the head-and-shoulders sets of kings and queens of the previous generation, and, like them, could be displayed to superb decorative effect in Long Galleries and state rooms. Many of the painters who produced them were of no more than indifferent quality, some working from workshops where a number of more or less specialist painters collaborated on the task of assembling the portraits: the face-painter, the drapery-painter, the painter of curtains and carpets, and, on occasion, the painter who added any heraldry or inscription. Following the example of Gheeraerts, canvas rather than panel was now the usual support: light-weight and in every way more practical for works on this scale.

Throughout his long career Gheeraerts's style remained virtually unchanged, and, though for a time he was patronised by the Queen, Anne of Denmark, in his later years his clientele came much more from the middle ranks of the aristocracy, the gentry (as for instance Lady Scudamore), and the universities. The learned James I's tastes were more traditional than those of his wife, and he patronised Gheeraerts's uncle, John de Critz (*c.*1552–1642), a copy of whose portrait of the King is at Montacute (82), as well as the characteristically conservative *1st Earl of Dorset* (28).

Anne of Denmark was an enthusiastic and extravagant patron of the arts, best known for the court masques which Ben Jonson and Inigo Jones created for her. Before she died she succeeded in attracting to her service Paul van Somer (*c.*1577/8–1622), the first of a new generation of painters to arrive in England from the Netherlands. His portraits, of which the formidable full-length family group of the *1st Earl of Monmouth and his Family* (73) is almost certainly a fine example, heralded the beginnings of an aesthetic revolution at court, and

The 'Ditchley' portrait of Elizabeth I; by Marcus Gheeraerts the Younger, c.1592 (National Portrait Gallery)

the return of the 'shadowed' manner. Anne's son, Henry, Prince of Wales, who shared her tastes, had also tired of the older generation of painters like Gheeraerts and his own court painter Robert Peake the Elder, and was at the time of his death negotiating for the services of Michiel van Miereveldt (1567–1641), one of the most accomplished exponents of the Dutch pre-baroque style. Miereveldt never came to England, but he was popular with English visitors to the Netherlands from about 1610, while among his later sitters are *Dudley Carleton, Viscount Dorchester* (78), diplomat and connoisseur, and soldiers like *Sir John Borlase* (93) and *Lord Vere of Tilbury* (96). Often quite modest in format, Miereveldt's portraits yet have a grasp of likeness and feeling for character which must have

(73) The 1st Earl of Monmouth and his Family; attributed to Paul van Somer, c.1617

made his English contemporaries seem utterly pedestrian.

The death of Henry, Prince of Wales in 1612 was a shattering blow to the morale of the nation, which saw in him the image of the perfect Renaissance prince. He was, however, succeeded by his brother Prince Charles, who was to become the greatest of all the Stuarts as a patron of the Arts. At Montacute is one of the most precocious of portraits of the young Prince. This is the full-length by the Flemish artist Abraham van Blyenberch (fl.1617–22) (59), who is recorded in London between 1617 and 1621, and who also painted a portrait of Ben Jonson (87) for the royal favourite, George Villiers, Duke of Buckingham. The young Prince evidently made a somewhat gangly sitter, and in format and accessories – table, curtain, columns and a token glimpse of landscape – the portrait hardly strays outside the usual Jacobean formula. However, there are differences in treatment, notably in the bold baroque forms of the drapery which encircles the columns behind the Prince, and in the exquisite little landscape with figures which foreshadows the poetic landscapes of Rubens, so different from the painted backdrops of Gheeraerts or Peake.

As king, Charles's patronage began with Daniel Mytens (c.1590–1647), who had come to England at about the same time as Blyenberch; certainly he was in London by 1618, when he painted the portraits of the Earl of Arundel and his wife. Born in Delft, his style formed under the influence of painters such as Miereveldt and Jan Anthonisz. van Ravesteyn, Mytens is chiefly responsible for introducing the Dutch manner into English painting, and his *Sir Thomas Edmondes* (57), painted c.1620, quite early in his stay, illustrates those qualities of sureness of form, refinement of technique and seriousness of mood which distinguish his work. He painted James I in 1621, and the King granted him an annual pension in 1624. In 1625, soon after his accession, Charles I appointed him one of his official 'picture-drawers of our Chamber in ordinarie' for life, and Mytens was to dominate court portraiture for almost a decade, until his departure from England in 1634.

Undoubtedly the foreign artists who came to England influenced the work of native artists. One

(59) Charles I; attributed to Abraham van Blyenberch, c.1617–20

of the most distinguished and prolific of these was Cornelius Johnson (1593–1661), born in London of Flemish parents who had fled Antwerp to avoid religious persecution. Johnson's early work is close in style to Gheeraerts, but he very quickly absorbed the Anglo-Dutch influence. Between his earliest dated works of 1617 and his departure from England in the Civil War in 1643, he produced a stream of distinguished portraits, mostly of the lower aristocracy and gentry, and mostly head and shoulders on panel or canvas in a feigned stone or marble oval. Almost all are signed and dated, so it is possible to chart Johnson's stylistic development closely, and indeed, in a modest way, to track the changes in English costume. There are three of these

An Unknown Man; by Cornelius Johnson, 1636
(Crimson Bedroom)

he was on a diplomatic business, he found time to paint a number of portraits and other works. Four years later, in 1632, the Dutch artist Hendrick Gerritsz. Pot painted the King and Queen, and among his other sitters was *Sir Robert Phelips* of Montacute (Great Hall). Sir Robert is the subject of a notably engaging and direct portrait, modest in ambition and wholly Dutch in flavour.

The great arrival of 1632, however, was Rubens's star pupil Anthony Van Dyck. Supremely talented and assured, Van Dyck brought to England for the first time all the splendours of the international baroque portrait, and he straightaway eclipsed all his rivals. Even Mytens could not compete, and returned to Holland in 1634. There are no portraits by Van Dyck at Montacute, and it is therefore not possible to assess fully there the glamour, movement and drama which he brought to portraiture in England, whether in his great equestrian portraits of the King, his ambitious family groups or his noble full-lengths. Nevertheless, there is some evidence of his influence on his contemporaries, among them Cornelius Johnson. In his three-quarter-length por-

head-and-shoulders portraits by him at Montacute. All have lost their true identities, but at one time or another have had distinguished names optimistically attached to them: a common problem with sixteenth- and seventeenth-century portraits. The *Unknown Man*, formerly considered a self-portrait (Crimson Bedroom), is an especially refined example of his work on this scale.

Among other foreign visitors was the Dutch Caravaggesque painter Gerrit van Honthorst (1590–1656), who was in England in 1628. He painted for the King the huge allegorical *Apollo and Diana* which now hangs at Hampton Court, and a group portrait of the *Duke of Buckingham and his Family*, of which a good early version is at Montacute (84). In this the dramatic lighting, lively colouring and the excited movement of the baby all testify to the effect of the new baroque style in portraiture which was in vogue on the Continent. The group speaks of confidence and prosperity only weeks before the Duke's assassination. In the following year Rubens visited London, and, although

(88) ? Nicholas Oudart; by William Dobson, c.1645

(84) The 1st Duke of Buckingham and his Family; after Gerrit van Honthorst, 1628

trait of the *1st Baron Coventry* in Parliamentary robes (62), a late work, Johnson shows a style clearly modified by knowledge of Van Dyck. This is most evident in the implied movement of Coventry's body, the full-blown baroque exuberance in the treatment of his robes, and the wholly Vandyckian brocade curtain which adds sparkle and movement to the background. Another English painter, William Dobson (1611–46), arguably the finest before Hogarth, is said to have worked in Van Dyck's studio, though there is no concrete evidence of this. Even in quite a modest (and damaged) work as his *?Nicholas Oudart* (88), formerly known as the poet Francis Quarles, Van Dyck's influence may be seen in the elegant disposition of the hands, the swag of drapery in the crook of his arm, and the slanting tree which dominates the glimpse of landscape beyond.

Van Dyck's influence continues like a breath of fresh air in British painting right through the seventeenth century, and was revived again by Gainsborough late in the eighteenth. It was he who, in the words of his contemporary William Sanderson, first 'put Ladies dresse into a careless Romance', and his portraits, relaxed and elegant, are the very antithesis of the stiff and bejewelled icons of the Elizabethan and Jacobean periods.

CHAPTER SIX
THE TEXTILES

In the late sixteenth century, textiles of varying sorts formed a vital part of the decoration and furnishing of any great house. They served a wide variety of purposes: as wall-coverings, bed-hangings, table-carpets and cushion covers. They could be deployed to superb decorative effect, but were also effective in excluding draughts and ensuring privacy. Montacute was no exception, and the inventory of 1638, taken at the death of Sir Robert Phelips, records the wealth of textiles in the house. The present Library, for instance, then the Great Chamber or 'Dininge Roome', contained '8 peice of arras [tapestry] hanginges, 1 fine arras carpet with armes . . . 2 turkie carpettes', as well as upholstery, often with gold and silk fringes or lace, and curtains. The Hall Chamber, in addition to tapestries, contained a 'guilt Bedstead with its furniture of Purple sattin imbroidered with shipps the curtaines and counterpart [counterpane] of wrought sattin faced with gold lace'; a chair, two stools and a footstool with cushion were all embroidered 'suitable to the tester of the bed'. Tradition has it that the Montacute tapestries were sold at the time of the Civil War to raise funds for the King, and all the domestic textiles originally in the house have disappeared. Among twentieth-century acquisitions, however, the Gamlen bed of 1612 in the Crimson Bedroom now has late seventeenth-century crewelwork hangings and cover, which, although not contemporary and no doubt less magnificent than the originals, yet give an idea of the way in which such a bed would have been dressed in the period.

Although the originals are long gone, Montacute today is rich in tapestries, thanks to the generosity of Sir Malcolm Stewart. Outstanding among these is the earliest in the collection, the *millefleurs* tapestry representing a knight on horseback against a background of flowers (hence the term *millefleurs*), which hangs in the Dining Room. This rare and highly decorative piece was commissioned by the town of Tournai in 1477–9 as a gift to the Governor of the Dauphiné, Jean de Daillon, Seigneur de Lude, whose coat of arms is in the top left corner. The heraldic wolf on the knight's banner may have formed part of the crest of de Daillon, but no satisfactory solution has yet been proposed for the initials 'JE' which accompany it. The tapestry was woven in the workshop of Wuillaume Desreumaulx, *tapissier* of Tournai, and is one of very few surviving examples from the late fifteenth century which may be precisely identified. It is a type of late Gothic tapestry particularly popular in its day, and similar pieces belonged to that avid English collector Henry VIII, who had at Hampton Court '1 odde pece of Tapistrie having on it a man pictured in harneys [harness or armour] on horsebake'. Needless to say, it is probably more magnificent than any of those formerly at Montacute.

Also from the late fifteenth century is the Flemish tapestry representing *The Eleventh Labour of Hercules, 'The Apples of the Hesperides'*, which hangs on the Staircase. The scenes depicted, against a *millefleurs* background, are (top): Hercules kills Busiris, the evil King of Egypt, and sacrifices him on the altar of Zeus, on which he had slain so many of his own victims; (bottom left): Hercules wrestles and kills the giant Antaeus without allowing him to touch his mother, the Earth, from whom he gained his strength; (bottom right): Hercules kills the dragon Ladon, guardian of the golden apples. Attempts to link the tapestry with a payment made in 1498 by a merchant of Oudenaarde to the Tournai painter Pierre Ferret for two cartoons for tapestries representing *The History of Hercules* have not been successful, and, though there are related pieces in Brussels, Paris and in the Burrell Collection, Glasgow, its place of manufacture has to date defied identification. In its compressed narrative style it is

'Millefleurs' tapestry commissioned by the tapestry-making town of Tournai in 1477–9 as a gift to Jean de Daillon, whose coat of arms appears in the top left corner (Dining Room)

The early eighteenth-century seat furniture in the Parlour is embroidered with mythological scenes

characteristic of its period, though the choice of a classical subject is comparatively novel.

The collection contains three good sixteenth-century tapestries of religious subjects. The earliest is *The Descent from the Cross*, on the Staircase, woven in Brussels *c.*1500–10, a scene of intense emotion, in which the boldly modelled drapery-forms recall the work of Gothic sculptors. Also on the Staircase and woven in Brussels, about the middle of the sixteenth century, is the panel of scenes from the apocryphal *Book of Tobias*. The compressed episodes are difficult to disentangle, but the main picture is of the younger Tobias returning home with his bride, Sara, preceded by the Archangel Raphael and his dog. In the background, Tobias and the angel are seen at Rages, greeting Raguel, the father of Sara. Other tapestries of the story of Tobias are in Vienna and Madrid. The third panel, which hangs in the Crimson Bedroom, represents *The Virgin, St John the Baptist and St Claudius*, and was woven in south Germany in the first half of the century. It is smaller in scale than the other two pieces, and represents a more austere and less dramatic interpretation of the late Gothic style. St Claudius (d. *c.*699) was Bishop of Besançon. The only other sixteenth-century tapestries in the house are the two exquisite small pieces representing unicorns, woven in Paris, and now covering cushions in Lord Curzon's Bedroom.

The last of the tapestries from the Stewart bequest is of much later date. This is the magnificent panel of *The Hunter* from a series of eight entitled *La Nouvelle Tenture des Indes*, which hangs in the Parlour. This was designed by François Desportes *c.*1731, but based on an earlier set woven for Louis XIV at the Gobelins factory in Paris. The cartoons for this first set were made from materials which had been presented to the King by Prince Maurice of Nassau in 1678. These comprised collections of ethnographic material made in South America and Africa for the Dutch East India Company between 1633 and 1644. Desportes's cartoons for the new series were exhibited at the Salon in Paris between 1731 and 1741, and were based on the old series, but with certain modifications. Like the prototypes, they proved highly popular. The present example is dated 1788 and signed (bottom right) by the master-weaver James Neilson, a Scot who introduced many innovations at the Gobelins factory. A friend of the architect Robert Adam, he executed numerous commissions for Adam's English patrons. This piece is in especially fresh condition, and conveys well the exoticism of the series as a whole. However, Montacute in its period of occupation by the Phelips family is unlikely to have seen the splendid products of the French royal tapestry factory of Gobelins.

Shown in the Parlour is a set of early eighteenth-century parcel gilt walnut seat furniture with particularly fine embroidered upholstery. The backs depict vaguely mythological scenes – figures in classical robes against chinoiserie landscapes – set within strapwork frames, with an outer border of flowers, fruit and leaves. The faces, worked on linen with tiny stitches, are exquisite examples of the embroiderer's craft. The seats are embroidered with flowers as, it was said, it was not thought proper in the eighteenth century to sit on the image of another human being. The uniformity of the stitch suggests that the embroidery was professionally done, but its exact origin is unknown.

It is difficult to overestimate the part played by needlework in the life of upper-class households from the sixteenth century onwards. It was generally the most popular leisure activity for the mistress of the house, her daughters and maids, the most delightful and productive way of filling 'those vacant hours which were not filled by devotion or business'. In this the fashion was set from the very top of society, and both Queen Mary and her sister Queen Anne were enthusiastic needlewomen. Of the former Bishop Burnet wrote that weak eyesight 'obliged her to resort to female handiwork in her desire to avoid idleness . . . She wrought with her own hands, and sometime with so constant a diligence, as if she had been to earn her bread by it. It was a new thing and looked a sight to see a Queen work so many hours a day.' This huge domestic industry is evoked at Montacute by the Goodhart Collection of samplers, from which changing selections are displayed in the Clifton Maybank Corridor. This was formed by Dr Douglas Goodhart over a period of some thirty years, and ranges in date from the early seventeenth century to the

Linen sampler, embroidered by Anna Peryn, 1681
(Goodhart Collection)

twentieth. He generously bequeathed the collection to the National Trust on his death.

The history of the sampler in this country goes back to at least 1500, when it was certainly not a child's piece (as it was later to become), but a cloth on which adult embroiderers kept stitches and patterns for trial and reference: the term 'sampler' derives from 'exampler' (the Old French 'essamplaire'). In sixteenth-century England domestic needlework flourished as never before, and the sampler became for the amateur needlewoman an invaluable tool. Samplers were important enough to be listed in inventories and bequeathed in wills. They were seen as a means of passing on designs and stitches to the next generation, and, indeed, their role was to become increasingly educational, as is underlined by the number of alphabetical samplers (the oldest in the collection is of 1627).

The earliest dated sampler in the collection, worked by Mary Quelch in 1609, is on parchment, but generally seventeenth-century examples are worked on plain-weave linens. They fall broadly into two types – 'band' and 'spot' samplers – in both of which the collection is rich. Band samplers are usually of long, narrow form, and feature bands of border patterns, worked one under the other. Many show a wide variety of whitework techniques, sometimes in association with cutwork borders, while others use polychrome silks and metal threads to achieve an effect of greater richness. Small human figures known as 'boxers' sometimes appear in these borders. Spot samplers are distinguished by the use of detached motifs, scattered apparently haphazardly over the surface, and suggesting a repertoire of designs intended for use. Some fall into a formula: a group of naturalistic motifs in the upper part and bands of repeating pattern below. Unlike band samplers, they are only rarely dated. Favourite motifs are sprays of flowers, birds and animals, insects and mermaids, usually worked in tent stitch. Border patterns exhibit a far wider range of stitches – eyelets, Gobelin, Hungarian, double-running and rococo – often enriched with silver and silver-gilt thread, and occasionally with spangles and beads.

In the eighteenth century, samplers took on a squarer shape with the abandonment of the band form, and from *c.*1750 onwards are often framed with a border. Such works were intended to be displayed and admired, rather than as objects of practical reference. Numerals and lettering assume greater prominence, and the range of stitches is much narrower. From *c.*1725 the plain-weave wool called 'tammy cloth' is generally the support. In the later part of the century many miniature samplers were produced, as well as darning and map samplers – these last are generally on commercially prepared white satin on which the map was already outlined.

Most characteristic of the nineteenth century are the verse samplers, with their borders of stylised birds, animals, flower pots and so on, usually worked in cross-stitch. The four 'In Memoriam' samplers in the collection intensify the note of youthful piety which suffuses the examples of this period. Most are worked in simple cross-stitch, a sad reflection of the decline in needlework skills in the period.

Another linen sampler, embroidered with coloured silks, from the Goodhart Collection, 1662

PLANS OF THE HOUSE

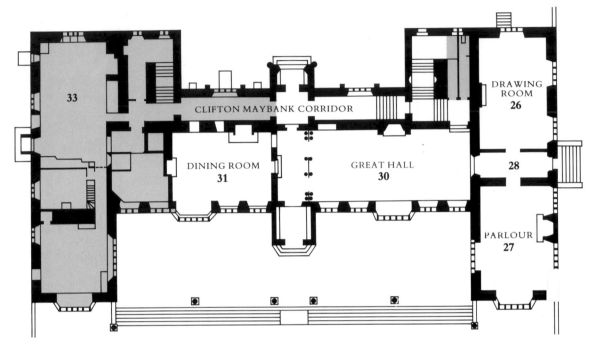

GROUND FLOOR

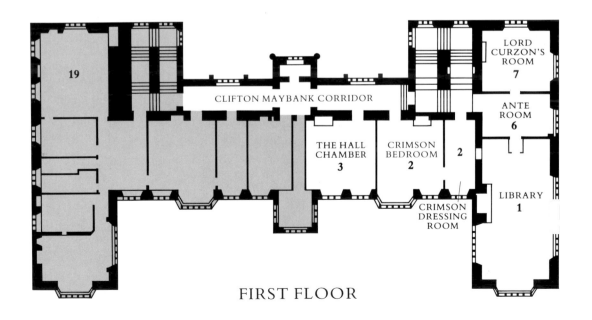

FIRST FLOOR

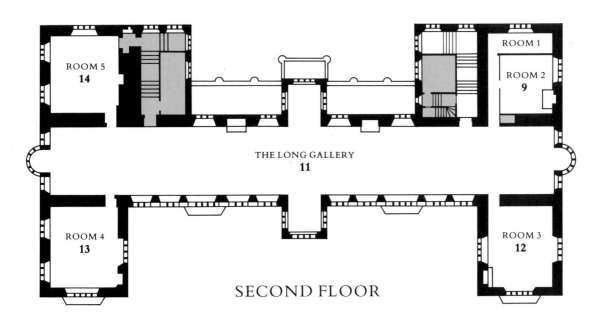

ROOM 5
14

ROOM 1

ROOM 2
9

THE LONG GALLERY
11

ROOM 4
13

ROOM 3
12

SECOND FLOOR

Areas of the house shaded grey on the plans are not shown to visitors

Suggested identification with rooms listed in 1638 Inventory

1 Dininge Roome
2 withdrawinge roome
3 best Chamber
4 Closset within ye best chamber
5 inner chamber to the best chamber
6 Lobbie without ye dininge Roome
7 garden chamber
8 chamber at top of the great stairs on the right hand
9 white chamber
10 Chamber within ye white chamber
11 Gallerie
12 primrose chamber

13 blew bedd chamber
14 wainscott chamber
15 mens chamber top of the house
16 Lobbie by ye little dininge Roome
17 Little dininge Roome
18 two little roomes within ye last roome
19 Kitchen chamber
20 Inner chamber
21 Larder chamber
22 clossett within ye Chamber
23 midle chamber
24 clossett within

25 Butlers chamber
26 Parlor chamber
27 Parlor
28 Lobbie by the Parlor
29 Cellar
30 Hall
31 Butterie & Cellar
32 Lobbie by the Kitchen
33 Kitchen
34 pastrie
35 drie Larder
36 wett Larder

CHAPTER SEVEN
THE HOUSE

THE APPROACH

In the seventeenth century, visitors approached from the main road which ran parallel to the front of the house, through a gatehouse into the east court. Today the path to the house skirts the south side, and emerges in the south-west corner of the east court, with its extensive lawn and herbaceous borders. A flight of six steps leads up to the stone terrace immediately in front of the house, flanked on the east side by six free-standing Doric columns supporting electric lights.

THE EAST FRONT

The three-storeyed east front is unaltered since the house was built in the last decade of the sixteenth century. It consists of a block of eleven bays, with a central frontispiece containing the main entrance, and more prominently projecting wings of a single bay topped by florid Flemish gables. Below the mullioned and transomed windows on the ground floor are pairs of empty shell-headed niches, and below those on the first floor further, undecorated, hemispherical niches. There are bay windows on both the ground and first floors, symmetrically placed flanking the central frontispiece, and in the end wings. These are capped by segmental pediments above the first-floor entablature. Between the windows of the top storey are further shell-headed niches containing full-length statues in classical dress of the Nine Worthies – Joshua, David, Judas Maccabaeus, Hector, Alexander, Julius Caesar, King Arthur, Charlemagne and Godfrey of Bouillon – which have been recently conserved. The roof line is enlivened by a balustrade, which is decorated with obelisks, and runs round the central block and the returns of the wings.

The arms above the entrance porch are those of the builder of the house, Sir Edward Phelips (1560?–1614), and incorporate, on the scroll at the bottom, the date 1601, the year, it is assumed, that the house was completed. Above the front door within is the welcoming inscription:

Through this wide op'ning Gate
None come too Early none Return too Late.

This should be read in association with the similar inscription over the door in the west front:

And yours my friends.

Both were probably put up in the nineteenth century in sententious allusion to the hospitality offered indoors, and are adapted from Alexander Pope's *Second Satire of the Second Book of Horace, Paraphrased*, with complete disregard for their context and prophetic irony for the Phelips family, for they come from the speech of an extravagant upper-class ne'er-do-well:

Pairs of empty shell-headed niches enliven the ground floor of the east front

My lands are sold, my Father's house is gone;
I'll hire another's, is not that my own,
And yours my friends? thro' whose free-opening gate
None comes too early, none departs too late.

The panelled oak front door opens into the Screens Passage.

THE SCREENS PASSAGE

This bisects the house. To the right lies the Hall and to the left the present Dining Room, originally the first of the series of domestic offices leading to the kitchen. This layout, medieval in origin, was standard in Elizabethan houses, and still functions in a number of Oxford and Cambridge colleges.

PAINTING

ABOVE THE WEST DOOR:

Sir Edward Phelips (1560?–1614)

The builder of the house, with his mace and seal bag as Speaker of the House of Commons. Though dated 1610, it was probably painted in the late seventeenth or early eighteenth century, based on an earlier portrait.
Unknown artist.

THE DINING ROOM

This takes its origins from the much smaller 'Butterie', which had a cellar below and a passage along the west side linking the Hall with the kitchen. Here wine and beer were dispensed by the butler under the supervision of the clerk of the kitchen. In 1787 Edward Phelips converted this small room into a 'Common Parlour', incorporating the passageway which had been made redundant by his new west corridor.

The room underwent its final metamorphosis about 1915 when Lord Curzon almost doubled its size by demolishing the partition which separated it from the adjoining room to the south (with bay window), thus creating the present dining-room.

CHIMNEY-PIECE

A concoction of Elizabethan and later elements, the chimney-piece was probably put together in the 1780s. It incorporates a plasterwork panel with the Phelips arms and motto *Pro aris et focis* (For homes and hearths) and the date 1599, perhaps reused from elsewhere in the house, flanked by a medley of ornamental woodwork and topped with a plaster cartouche bearing the head of a woman, which is apparently late seventeenth-century in date.

PAINTINGS

Edward VI (1537–53)
Only legitimate son of Henry VIII, by Jane Seymour; reigned 1547–53. A version of a portrait in the Royal Collection painted for Henry VIII shortly before his death, and sometimes unsatisfactorily attributed to William Scrots. For another portrait see no. 4 in Room 1 on the second floor.
Unknown artist, perhaps seventeenth century.

Robert Dudley, Earl of Leicester (1532?–88)
Favourite of Elizabeth I and a 'light and greedy man' (see below, no. 21).
Unknown artist, perhaps after Steven van der Meulen (fl.1543–68).

Unknown Man
According to the inscription, aged 26 in 1604. Formerly attributed to Marcus Gheeraerts the Younger, but probably Dutch.
Unknown artist, 1604.

Mary, Queen of Scots (1542–87)
Inscribed with the date 1585 and age 42, but almost certainly deriving from a miniature by Nicholas Hilliard probably of 1578. The Queen had been a prisoner of Elizabeth I for ten years when the original miniature was painted.
Unknown artist, probably after Nicholas Hilliard (1547/8–1618/19), 1578.

Thomas Cavendish (1560–92)
Buccaneer and the second Englishman to circumnavigate the world (1586–8). He wears a pearl-encrusted cloak and ropes of pearls as a sash. (Stewart bequest.)
English School, late sixteenth century.

Elizabeth Knollys, Lady Layton
Wife of Sir Thomas Layton of Guernsey; maid of honour to Elizabeth I; sister to Lettice, who married as his second wife Robert Dudley, Earl of Leicester (see below) in 1578. Among many jewels, in her hair is one in the form of a starfish and corals; at her breast is a pendant with a dove and snake, emblems of mildness and prudence respectively. Above her coat of arms (left) are her initials, flanking the family crest, an elephant. (Stewart bequest.)
Attributed to George Gower (c.1540?–96), 1577.

The chimney-piece in the Dining Room was probably put together from a number of different elements in the 1780s

TAPESTRY

The room is dominated by the late fifteenth-century *millefleurs* tapestry representing a knight on horseback against a background of flowers, which hangs on the south wall. It was woven in the workshop of Wuillaume Desreumaulx of Tournai, and is one of very few surviving examples from the period which may be precisely identified. (See Chapter Six for further details.)

FURNITURE

In 1834 the furnishings of this room included two dining-tables, a dumb waiter, a plate warmer and six mahogany chairs, together with a sofa, two easy chairs, four wicker chairs, a card-table, a tea magazine and an ottoman.

The furniture today dates mainly from the sixteenth and seventeenth centuries, and includes the sixteenth-century Italian walnut refectory table, two elm and walnut X-frame folding chairs (against the south wall), whose design derives from fifteenth-century prototypes, and a 'press' or 'ambry' oak cupboard with panels carved in Gothic style, and a walnut 'Nonsuch' chest, so-called because of the design of its inlay of holly, bog-oak and various coloured woods, which resembles illustrations of Henry VIII's Nonsuch Palace near Cheam in Surrey. Around the table are five Cromwellian 'farthingale' chairs with leather seats and backs, and, at the table ends, two Jacobean oak armchairs, one with bog-oak inlay.

CERAMICS AND GLASS

The table is set with part of a late eighteenth-century Chinese export dinner service and mainly late eighteenth- and early nineteenth-century glass. The Sheffield plate double coaster holds two rare late eighteenth-century decanters with compartments for ice (later stoppers).

On leaving the Dining Room, return via the Screens Passage to the Great Hall.

THE GREAT HALL

In medieval times the Great Hall was the principal, often the only, room of a house, invariably rising to the roof timbers; here the lord, his family and servants lived together. From the mid-fourteenth century, however, the family increasingly ate in other rooms, while the servants remained in the hall. This diminishing enthusiasm for communal eating continued through the sixteenth century, and at Montacute, by the end of the seventeenth century, a servants' dining-room had been made in the south wing. The comparatively modest scale of the Montacute hall is explained partly by this trend and partly by the technical difficulty of building a

room more than one storey high in the centre of a house of such narrow section. In Jacobean times the Hall would have been used as a communal living-room, and in 1638 furnishings included forms, tables and shovel-board table. It still, however, needed to impress, for here the head of the family received his guests, and here began the formal procession of food from the kitchen to the Great Chamber (now the Library) on the first floor.

SCREEN

At the south end of this impressive room is a single-storey screen of some elaboration, with columns, rusticated arches and strapwork entablature. The comparatively crudely modelled figures of the entablature contrast with the finely carved rams' heads of the capitals of the columns, a motif which owes its sophistication to foreign pattern books.

PLASTERWORK

The north wall of the Hall is decorated with an early seventeenth-century plasterwork panel depicting (left) a hen-pecked husband having a quick drink while minding the baby; his exceedingly unattrac-

The grand stone screen separates the Great Hall from the Screens Passage and the Kitchen offices beyond; watercolour by C. J. Richardson, 1834

The 'Stang Ride' plasterwork in the Great Hall

tive wife catches him in the act and hits him with a shoe. The incident is observed by a neighbour, who no doubt reports the incident to the village fathers, who condemn the luckless man to 'Riding the Stang' (above) – that is, to be paraded round the village astride a pole as an object of derision. The custom is referred to in Thomas Hardy's *The Mayor of Caster-bridge*, but its origins are mysterious.

PANELLING AND FIREPLACE

The ensemble of the Hall is completed by the original panelling and chimney-piece with its coupled Doric columns and triglyph frieze.

STAINED GLASS

The heraldic glass in the windows includes the coats of arms of Elizabeth I (centre) and Sir Edward Phelips and his brothers. One panel is dated 1599.

FLOOR

The present floor is the 'oak dancing floor properly sprung', which was installed in the late nineteenth century by William Robert Phelips. Six inches below this lies the original stone floor (it survives in the ground-floor Clifton Maybank Corridor), which was much admired by Thomas Coryate, who compared it favourably with the paving of St Mark's Square in Venice:

This part of the Piazza, together with all the other is fairly paved with brick, which maketh a shew fair enough; but had it been paved either with diamond pavier made of free stone, as the halls of some of our great Gentlemen in England are, (amongst the rest of my Honourable and thrice-worthy Maecenas Sir Edward Phillips, in his magnificent house of Monta-gue . . .) or with other pavier ex quadrato lapide, which we call Ashler, in Somersetshire, certainly it

would have made the whole Piazza much more glorious and resplendent than it is.

PAINTINGS

In 1828 J.P. Neale saw family portraits hanging here, together with 'A Boar Piece and a Dog' by Snyders and 'Cattle Pieces' by Beach. It is still hung with family portraits.

ON THE SCREEN:

Sir Robert Phelips (1586–1638)
Son of the builder of Montacute; a distinguished Parliamentarian. The portrait has been reduced in size, and once bore the motto 'Otros tiempos: otros cuydados' (other times, other thoughts), the date 1632 and the age of the sitter, 47. Phelips holds a paper inscribed: 'Mr Egertons Petitio[n]. Read and referred to the Committee for Courts of Justice.', in allusion to the sitter's chairmanship of the committee of enquiry into the charges of corruption brought against Lord Chancellor Bacon in 1621. This portrait is painted over a religious picture, and the head of what may be the Virgin can dimly be perceived above Sir Robert's own. The Dutch artist Pot was in London in 1632.
Attributed to Hendrik Gerritsz. Pot (*c.*1585–1657), 1632.   NPG

WEST WALL (FACING WINDOWS):

Colonel Edward Phelips (*c.*1613–80)
Grandson of the builder, and a Royalist colonel in the Civil War. The composition is based on Van Dyck's portrait of Sir Edmund Verney (private collection).
Attributed to Jacob Huysmans (1633?–96), 1663.

Sir Edward Phelips (1638–99)
Son of the above.
Unknown artist, 1685.

Edward Phelips (1678–1734)
Nephew of the above and son of John Phelips (1644–1701). He married his cousins, first Ann, then Elizabeth, Phelips, daughters of the above. MP for Somerset, 1722. This is a three-quarter-length adaptation of the half-length portrait in the Parlour Passage attributed to Jonathan Richardson and dated 1730.
Unknown artist, partly after Jonathan Richardson (1665–1745), 1731.

Edith Phelips, Mrs Carew Mildmay (1694–1772)
The youngest daughter of Sir Edward Phelips (1638–99) and Edith Blake, she married Carew Hervey Mildmay, younger brother of the 1st Earl Fitzwalter, as his second wife in 1744. The *putti* in the portrait may represent still-born children, and one carries a bubble emblematic of the frailty of life. The Florentine Soldi came to London in 1736, and twice painted Mildmay, as well as doing work for his brother. The *putti* show the influence of another Italian artist, Amigoni, who had also worked for Lord Fitzwalter.
Andrea Soldi (*c.*1703–71), 1750.

Edward Phelips (1725–97)
Son of Edward Phelips (1678–1734) and builder of the new west front. He holds a letter addressed to him at Montacute and dated 1765. On the table are Locke's *Works* and Montesquieu's *Spirit of Laws.*
Unknown artist, 1765.

John Phelips (1784–1834)
Grandson of the above. A lithograph of the same sitter seated in the Great Hall also hangs on this wall (south end), and his chair is still by the screen. In the background of this print is Beach's portrait of his father, the Rev. William Phelips (1755–1806).
Unknown artist, *c.*1820–5.

Unknown Man
The maritime scene in the background suggests that the sitter had a connection with the sea.
Unknown artist, *c.*1730.

FURNITURE

The oak refectory table with cup-and-cover legs, its frame inlaid with yew and sycamore, is English, *c.*1590 (lent by Trinity College, Oxford). Ranged against the west wall are (left of the fireplace): six walnut dining-chairs in Dutch style of *c.*1700, and (right) five high-back caned chairs of Charles II period. Oak furniture against the east wall includes a side-table dated 1657, a table-bench with tip-up top, also seventeenth-century, two Elizabethan armchairs, and (north end) a child's chair dated 1635. Collections of pewter (some early eighteenth-century) and copper are also displayed here.

THE PARLOUR PASSAGE

The door in the north wall contains a nineteenth-century stained-glass panel of the Phelips arms.

PAINTINGS

WEST (LEFT-HAND) WALL:

Edward Tenison (1673–1735)
Cousin of Thomas Tenison, Archbishop of Canterbury; Bishop of Ossory, 1731–5. A version of Kneller's portrait, dated 1720, belonging to Corpus Christi College, Cambridge.
Attributed to Sir Godfrey Kneller (1646–1723), *c.*1720.

(?) Bridget Phelips, Lady Napier (1707–58)
Inscribed on the book which she holds with the name 'Dame Bridget Phelips' and the date 1670. However, the portrait is clearly of much later date. Attributed to John Vanderbank (1694?–1739), *c.*1720–30.

John Phelips (1644–1701)
Second son of Colonel Edward Phelips (*c.*1613–80), of Kilpatrick, Co. Cork and London.
Unknown artist, *c.*1690.

NORTH (END) WALL:

William Phelips (1823–89)
Eldest grandson of the Rev. William Phelips. There is a view of Montacute in the background.
Thomas Musgrove Joy (1812–66), signed and dated 1858.

EAST (RIGHT-HAND) WALL:

William Phelips (d.1714)
Third son of Colonel Edward Phelips (*c.*1613–80).
Unknown artist, 1700.

Sir Thomas Egerton, Viscount Brackley (1540?–1617)
Lord Chancellor, 1603–17; with his seal bag as Lord Keeper to Elizabeth I, whose arms and initials it bears.
Unknown artist, between 1596 and 1603.

Right, off the Parlour Passage, is the Parlour.

THE PARLOUR

In the early seventeenth century the family generally ate in the 'Parlour', and used the 'Dininge Roome' above only on formal occasions. There was also a 'Little Dininge Roome' on the first floor. All these rooms were quite remote from the kitchen in the south-west wing, and it is not surprising that before the middle of the century a new 'little parlour' had been created much nearer to it. In 1728 the present Parlour was furnished with a tea-table, two card-tables, 'twenty four Turky work't Chairs' and two large looking glasses. In the nineteenth century it was for a time a dining-room once again, before metamorphosis into a billiard room. Despite these changes of use, it retains its chief features.

CHIMNEY-PIECE

The massive chimney-piece on the north wall is of Ham Hill stone. The strapwork lozenge in the middle of the upper register once contained a plaster profile medallion, reputedly a portrait of Edward Phelips (1725–97) – a casualty of Curzon's tenancy.

PLASTERWORK

The plaster frieze, dating from the early seventeenth century, represents a procession of engagingly naive animals, including a camel, interspersed with the Phelips arms and strapwork.

A detail of the Parlour plasterwork frieze

PANELLING

The wainscoting is probably also original. The room was described as 'wainscoted' in 1667, and was drawn by C.J.Richardson in the 1830s as a good example of Elizabethan panelling. However, there have been modifications: the south window has been filled in and panelled, and the entrance remodelled.

PAINTING

The Children of Charles I
On loan from Stourhead House, Wiltshire.
After Van Dyck (1599–1641).

TAPESTRY

On the south wall hangs a fine Gobelins tapestry of *The Hunter* from a series of eight entitled *La Nouvelle Tenture des Indes*, designed by François Desportes *c*.1731, but based on an earlier set woven for Louis XIV (see Chapter Six for further details).

FURNITURE

A walnut bureau with seaweed marquetry of various woods, English or Dutch, early eighteenth century.
A set of chairs and settee with parcel gilt walnut frames and contemporary covers embroidered in *gros* and *petit point* (*c*.1722) with mythological figures on the backs and flowers on the seats, from Chicheley House, Buckinghamshire (see Chapter Six).
The late eighteenth-century Gothick longcase clock has a movement by James Moule.

Leave the Parlour and cross the Parlour Passage to the Drawing Room.

THE DRAWING ROOM

Before 1651 Colonel Edward Phelips promoted this room from a bedroom to be his 'round parlour', so-called perhaps because of the 'round table board' recorded there in that year. This name lingered into the eighteenth century, but by 1778 it had become the drawing-room, and, by the time of the 1834 inventories, the 'Great Drawing Room'. In the 1880s William Robert Phelips and his second wife, Constance Ponsonby-Fane, redecorated it, again as a drawing-room, to display their wedding presents,

'The Hunter', from a series of Gobelins tapestries designed by Françoise Desportes, c.1731 (Palrour)

which included an 'inlaid secretaire from Lady Stanley', a 'Red Ware flower pot from Hon. and Mrs H. de Grey', and 'Delft pots . . . given by E. Helyar' (mother-in-law). To keep these company, furniture was moved from elsewhere in the house, such as 'the large inlaid Cabinet . . . from upstairs' and 'the copper wine cooler from the dining room'.

DECORATION

The panelling between the windows and the high dado date from the 1880s, and the room retains none of its original features. The marble chimney-piece, Neptune fireback and firedogs are from Coleshill, Berkshire, gutted by fire in 1952. The cartouche in the lintel is carved with the monogram of William Bouverie, who was created Earl of Radnor in 1765, surmounted by an earl's coronet. The flock wallpaper was introduced by the National Trust.

PAINTINGS

Sir William Heathcote, 3rd Bt (1746–1819),
The Rev. William Heathcote, and Major Vincent
Hawkins Gilbert out Hunting
A crowded composition of three men in hunt livery. Major Gilbert (centre), holding a fox's mask, wears a pink coat and was evidently the Master of Fox Hounds; Sir William (right) is in pink, his son the Rev. William (on horseback) in blue. Arguably the masterpiece in oils of this artist, who normally worked on a smaller scale in gouache and pastels. (Cook bequest.)
Daniel Gardner (1750?–1805), c.1790.

An Unknown Woman, by Sir Joshua Reynolds, c.1753 (Drawing Room)

Colonel Isaac Gale
Nothing is known of the sitter. (Stewart bequest.)
Sir Joshua Reynolds (1723–92), c.1763.

Sir Ralph Abercromby (1734–1801)
With Sir John Moore, the regenerator of the British army; served in the Seven Years War, and afterwards as an MP opposed the government's American policy; Commander-in-Chief in the West Indies, 1795–7, and in the Mediterranean, 1800; died of wounds after defeating the French at Alexandria. (Stewart bequest.)
John Hoppner (1758–1810), c.1799.

Summer Flowers
A decorative piece by an Antwerp artist whose work is close in style to that of his father. (Stewart bequest.)
Gaspar Peeter Verbrugghen the Younger (1664–1730). Signed and obscurely dated.

Unknown Girl
(Stewart bequest.)
Manner of Thomas Hudson (1701–79), 1750s.

Susan Murrill, Mrs Henry Hill (1717–94)
The sitter married Henry Hill in 1744, the year after he succeeded his father as Rector of Buxhall, Suffolk. An engaging portrait, painted in the artist's late Ipswich period, in a rococo frame. (Stewart bequest.)
Thomas Gainsborough (1727–88), late 1750s.

Unknown Woman
The sitter of this faintly theatrical portrait may perhaps be Elizabeth Hamilton, a cousin of the artist's early friend and patron, Captain John Hamilton RN, who married first Colonel John Cameron (1754) and secondly the Comte de Fay. It is in a fine rococo frame. (Stewart bequest.)
Sir Joshua Reynolds (1723–92), c.1753.

Anthony Francis Haldimand (1741–1817)
London merchant and founder of the banking house of Morris, Prevost & Co. (Stewart bequest.)
Sir Thomas Lawrence (1769–1830), c.1795–1800.

Captain Robert Boyle Nicholas (1744–80)
Post Captain on HMS *Thunderer*. In the background is Nicholas's yacht *Nepaul*. The seascape is perhaps by the marine painter Dominic Serres. (Stewart bequest.)
Francis Cotes (1726–70) and (?) Dominic Serres (1722–93), 1760s.

Unknown Man
Formerly said to be Lucius Cary, 2nd Viscount Falkland. (Stewart bequest.)
Cornelius Johnson (1593–1661), mid-1630s.

Old Man
Perhaps a nineteenth-century copy after Ribera (1591?–1652).

FURNITURE

The mahogany breakfront bookcase against the north wall dates from c.1790.
Part of a set of ten mahogany armchairs upholstered in red damask made by William Linnell for Sir Richard Hoare, 1st Bt of Barn Elms.
A pair of gilt-wood side-tables with eagle supports in the manner of William Kent, 1730s.
A walnut card-table with candle stands and counter wells, c.1715.
A Louis XIV Boulle writing-table, c.1700.

LEFT OF DOOR:

A late seventeenth-century lacquered cabinet on stand.

RIGHT OF DOOR:

A second lacquered cabinet on stand, of slightly later date than the other, *c.*1700.

CERAMICS

IN THE BOOKCASE:

Top shelf: Chinese *famille rose* plates.
Second shelf: more *famille rose* and pieces from a Ridgway porcelain tea service with blue and gold decoration (*c.*1820–5).
Third shelf: more Ridgway, a Meissen shaving dish (eighteenth-century) and Staffordshire figurines.
Fourth shelf: pieces from a nineteenth-century Worcester porcelain tea and coffee service, decorated with birds in foliage and gilded, and a Sèvres pen tray.
Bottom shelf: Worcester and Ridgway.

A Chinese 'Dog of Fo', K'ang Hsi period, 1662–1722 (Drawing Room)

ON THE CHIMNEY-PIECE:

Two Chinese porcelain figures of 'Ho-Ho' birds (Chi'en Lung period, 1736–95), a Japanese Arita carp, and two Wedgwood black basalt tripod urns.

FLANKING THE FIREPLACE:

A pair of Chinese 'Dogs of Fo' (K'ang Hsi period, 1662–1722).

ON THE LACQUER CABINETS:

A pair of Pontypool (painted tin) chestnut urns, early nineteenth-century.

Return to the Great Hall where the doorway on the right leads to the Staircase.

THE STAIRCASE

There are staircases in both the angles of the west front of Montacute, built of huge slabs of Ham stone on a rectangular plan, and running up in short flights round a central pier of solid masonry: a development of the circular newel staircase of medieval times. This, the North Staircase, is the principal one, which Sir Edward and his guests would have taken to the Great Chamber on the first floor. The steps, some of which are of solid blocks of stone, are 7 feet across; the central pier measures 5 feet by 12, and is decorated at intervals with shell-headed niches of the same form as those on the east front of the house, typical of the work of William Arnold. Visitors are welcome to use them as seats.

PAINTING

Unknown lady
Probably a member of the Phelips family.
Unknown artist, *c.*1650.

TAPESTRIES

On the lower part of the Staircase is hung an important tapestry from the bequest of Sir Malcolm Stewart: *The Eleventh Labour of Hercules, 'The Apples of the Hesperides'*, Flemish, late fifteenth-century (see Chapter Six).

Turning left at the first-floor landing, enter the Library Ante-Room, and turn left into Lord Curzon's Bedroom.

THE LIBRARY
(FORMERLY GREAT CHAMBER)

In this, his Great Chamber, Sir Edward Phelips would have received important visitors and dined in state, and it still has considerable impact on visitors as they enter. The Elizabethans dined at eleven in the morning and supped at five or six.

The history of the Montacute Great Chamber can be followed in successive inventories, extracts from which are set out in the Appendix. Evidently the early eighteenth century was a lean time for the family, and the Great Chamber, which would have been costly to heat, was closed up. By 1728 it was being used as a store room in which the family portraits were placed with 'other Lumber Goods'. In 1791 John Collinson refers to the room as the Library, and in the early nineteenth century it was crowded with oak library and other furniture, most of which was sold in 1834. In the following decade

William Phelips put in the plasterwork ceiling, altered the panelling and installed the bookpresses. Original Elizabethan features which survive are the chimney-piece, the plaster frieze and the stained glass. The internal porch, however, was not originally in the room, but in the Parlour below. It reached the Library by the 1830s, but was subsequently removed for use as a wardrobe, until reinstated by Lord Curzon. Elaborately carved and decorated, it bears the motto HOC AGE ('Do this').

CHIMNEY-PIECE

The Portland stone chimney-piece is the grandest in the house, the lower section flanked by pairs of Corinthian columns, and the overmantel by shell-headed niches. Chimney-pieces of similar design are at Wayford House, Somerset, Wolfeton House, Dorset, and at Stockton House in Wiltshire. They also share such distinctive features as the outsize egg-

The Library

(Opposite page)
The stained glass in the Library features the arms of the Phelips family, their allies, neighbours and rulers

The Library chimney-piece once contained statues of two nude women; watercolour by C. J. Richardson, 1834

number of scratched inscriptions in English and Latin of a pious and moralistic nature. All are attributed to Edward Phelips (1725–97) on the basis of one which is initialed EP and dated 1770:

To Virtue only & her friends a Friend,
The World besides may blame or may Commend,
All the Malicious Lies that World can raise
Disturb me not, I count it's Censure praise [:]

BOOKS

Books displayed in this room include the Phelips family Bible of 1717, in two volumes, bound in red calf.

FURNITURE

The most important furniture is the set of six walnut cane-back armchairs of early eighteenth-century design, one of which features in Richardson's watercolour of the Great Hall (*c.*1834). The only original furniture surviving at Montacute, they were bought back for the house through the generosity of the Trust's American arm, the Royal Oak Foundation. Note also the pair of mahogany gate-leg dining-tables (*c.*1750), and the mahogany library steps inlaid with tulipwood, box and ebony (*c.*1770).

METALWORK

The Limoges enamel candlesticks on one of the dining-tables are decorated with the monogram of Henry II of France and his mistress, Diane de Poitiers.

CARPET

The fawn and green Chenille carpet was formerly at Brockhampton Park, Herefordshire.

Return to the first-floor landing of the Staircase, where the door on the left leads into the Crimson Dressing Room.

THE CRIMSON DRESSING ROOM

Originally this room formed, with the following room, the 'withdrawinge roome' where on formal occasions Sir Edward Phelips and his guests would retire after dining in the Great Chamber. The door in the north wall linking it with the Great Chamber was soon walled up, and the presence of the state bed here in 1651 suggests that the Withdrawing Room

and-tongue moulding in the overmantel, and the strapwork decoration immediately above the fireplace opening, which echoes the cartouche above. In the middle of the Montacute overmantel is a small reclining female nude; Richardson's watercolour of *c.*1834 shows two statues of nude women in the flanking niches, but these, perhaps predictably, were removed in the Victorian era.

STAINED GLASS

The stained glass in this room (and in the Great Hall) is one of the most important features of the house – a rare survival – which must have delighted Sir Edward's guests with its brilliant colours and display of heraldry. There are 42 shields, made up in glass ovals: the heraldic achievements of the various branches of the Phelips family, their Somerset neighbours, powerful allies at court and, naturally, the Royal arms (centre). The glass was restored in the nineteenth century, and a few of the shields date from that time; they have again been conserved recently. In the glass of the east window are a had lost its original function by that date. The name, however, lingered, and the room was known as the 'Drawing Room' as late as 1728, when it had been a bedroom for more than seventy-five years. The partition which now forms the south wall of this dressing-room was probably erected by Edward Phelips in 1788, when he 'new papered' all the bedrooms which opened on to his new Clifton Maybank Corridor (see below). The present name is first found in the inventory of 1834, and probably derives from the crimson wallpaper, fragments of which were discovered during recent renovations.

PAINTINGS

The Visitation, with St Paul and St Francis
Somewhat in the style of the late fifteenth-century Florentine artist Bartolommeo di Giovanni.
Florentine school, fifteenth century.

The Holy Family with St John
Italian school, seventeenth century (?).

The Madonna and Child
With a later (now indistinct) inscription on the *cartellino*: *Joanes Baptista Choneglianensis* (ie the early sixteenth-century Venetian artist Cima di Coneg-liano). The painting's poor condition makes an attribution impossible.
Italian school, *c*.1500.

Landscape with Figures
A characteristic, though damaged Italianate work by this Dutch landscapist; formerly in the collection of the Earls of Derby. (Cook bequest.)
Nicolaes Berchem (1620–83), mid-seventeenth century.

FURNITURE

A Florentine *cassone* of *c*.1600, with caryatid herms at the corners and paw feet, and a leather-covered trunk, studded with nails in tulip patterns, late seventeenth century.
A pair of high back walnut chairs with crestings of cherubs, urns and flowers, Flemish, *c*.1670.
An oak chest of drawers, English, mid-seventeenth century.

CERAMICS

A maiolica dish from the Corradi factory, Albesoli, Genoa, *c*.1600, decorated with the figure of Bacchus, god of wine.

Continue into the Crimson Bedroom.

THE CRIMSON BEDROOM

This formed the larger part of the original 'with-drawinge roome' (see above). The early seventeenth-century plaster overmantel, inserted in the frieze, depicts *The Judgement of Paris*, a subject also found in overmantels at Wolfeton House, Dorset, and Dunster Castle in Somerset. It must once have been part of a more elaborate chimney-piece which has disappeared. The walls below the deep plaster-work frieze were once hung with tapestries. Both frieze and dado of this and the preceding room must have been adapted and extended at the time the two rooms were created out of one around 1788.

PAINTINGS

Unknown Woman
Traditionally but wrongly said to represent Mary, Queen of Scots.
French school, *c*.1560. NPG

Queen Jane (1509?-37)
Jane Seymour, third Queen of Henry VIII; mother of Edward VI; 'of middle stature and no great beauty, so fair that one would rather call her pale than otherwise'. The original is in Vienna.
After Hans Holbein (1497/8–1543), *c*.1539–40.

Unknown Woman
Wrongly identified as Catherine Howard, fifth Queen of Henry VIII, and more probably a member of the Cromwell family. The original is in Toledo, Ohio.
After Hans Holbein (1497/8–1543), *c*.1535–40.
NPG

Unknown Man
Formerly thought to be a self-portrait of the artist.
Cornelius Johnson (1593–1661), signed and dated 1636. NPG

Edward Hastings, Baron Hastings of Loughborough (d.1573)
Mary I's Master of the Horse; Lord Chamberlain, 1557; a staunch Roman Catholic; created a peer, 1558. Inscribed with the date 1573, his arms and motto: *veritas vi sua vice*. His book is inscribed in Latin: 'I am not ashamed of the witness of Christ'.
English school, 1573.

Unknown Man
Formerly thought to represent Richard Weston, 1st Earl of Portland.
Cornelius Johnson (1593–1661), signed and dated 1627. NPG

*The Crimson
Bedroom*

BED

The room is dominated by the massive oak bed, its ornate tester supported by posts boldly carved with variations on the cup-and-cover motif and acanthus leaves. The headboard is decorated with the coats of arms of James I (with his initials), flanked by those of his son, Henry, Prince of Wales, and son-in-law, Frederick V, Elector Palatine. The arms establish the date of the bed as 1612, the year in which Prince Henry died and the Elector came to England to marry James's only daughter, the Princess Elizabeth (later to be known as 'The Winter Queen'). The bed was given to the National Trust by Mr J.C.B. Gamlen, and is especially appropriate to Montacute, for Sir Edward Phelips was not only an officer in Prince Henry's household, but also organised the Masque of the Middle Temple, which formed part of Princess Elizabeth's wedding celebrations. The bed has late seventeenth-century crewelwork hangings and cover (remounted and not the originals).

OTHER FURNITURE

At the foot of the bed stands an oak chest with arched plank top and peg hinges, *c.*1500. Beside the bed is a walnut toilet glass (the upper mirror missing), similar to the 'New Patent Toilet Glass' for viewing the front and back of the head, illustrated in Heal's catalogue of 1887. The oak chest of drawers against the north wall is English and dated 1662, the front inlaid with bone and mother-of-pearl. An oak cabinet on stand, also inlaid with mother-of-pearl and of similar date, stands against the west wall. The pair of high-back walnut chairs and the elbow chair *en suite*, with crestings of cherubs, urns and flowers, are Charles II.

On the oak cabinet is a seventeenth-century mirror with a silk frame embroidered with animals, flowers and Old Testament characters.

CERAMICS

On the window sill is a maiolica dish dating from the sixteenth century, depicting *Moses striking the Rock*.

TAPESTRY

Over the fireplace hangs a tapestry of *The Virgin, St John the Baptist and St Claudius*, south German, first half of the sixteenth century.

Turn left into the Clifton Maybank Corridor.

THE CLIFTON MAYBANK CORRIDOR

This was added to the house by Edward Phelips (1725–97), and gives independent access to the rooms in the centre range of the house, which had previously been interconnected. At the south-east end an inspection shaft, cut into the wall, gives a glimpse of the original outside wall of the house and a window, and the wattle and daub of the present internal wall. On the west side is the small Parvis Room, looking out over the West Drive.

FURNITURE

Several seventeenth-century oak chests.

PICTURES

A small number of drawings and engravings of Montacute and its interior hang here, and in the Parvis Room a few early twentieth-century Phelips family photographs.

THE GOODHART COLLECTION OF SAMPLERS

Formed by the late Dr Douglas Goodhart over a period of some thirty years, they range in date from the early seventeenth to the twentieth century. For conservation reasons only a selection from the collection is shown each year. The display is labelled, and the history of the development of the sampler is described in Chapter Six.

Leading off the Clifton Maybank Corridor is the Hall Chamber.

THE HALL CHAMBER

Throughout the history of the house this room has always been a bedroom. Originally it was the 'best Chamber', but since 1651 has been known as the 'hall chamber'. It is unlikely that Sir Edward Phelips slept here, for this room would have been reserved for very grand visitors – an index of the owner's wealth and prestige. In 1638 it was filled with opulent furniture, tapestries and paintings, and had a 'great lookinge glasse', an outstandingly luxurious feature. The splendid plasterwork overmantel carries the arms of Sir Edward Phelips, the builder of Montacute, and his second wife Elizabeth Pigott (whose arms include three picks, in punning allusion to her name). The strapwork surround is also found in a chimney-piece at Wolfeton House.

PAINTINGS

A Young Girl
Unfinished. Formerly attributed to Raeburn. (Stewart bequest.)
English school, late eighteenth century.

'Master Sanders'
Nothing is known of the sitter. The portrait is said to be by 'P. J. Bone', but no artist of this name is recorded. It may be by Henry Bone (1779–1855). (Stewart bequest.)
Unknown artist, early nineteenth century.

TAPESTRY

The Descent from the Cross, Brussels, c.1500–10.

FURNITURE

The mahogany bed with carved posts of c.1750 is from Coleshill, Berkshire.
Below the tapestry is a French Renaissance oak buffet, highly carved with figures, leafy scrolls and linenfold panelling.

Return to the Staircase and take the stairs to the Long Gallery.

THE STAIRCASE

TEXTILES

On the inner wall is a modern needlework carpet copied from a mid-eighteenth-century example at Hatfield House in Hertfordshire, embroidered by Norah Sanders and completed after her death.

On the mezzanine landing hangs a mid-sixteenth-century Brussels tapestry illustrating scenes from the *Book of Tobias* (see Chapter Six). The main section shows Tobias returning home with his bride Sara, preceded by his dog and the Archangel Raphael.

THE LONG GALLERY

This impressive room extends the full length of the house, and, measuring 172 feet from oriel to oriel, is the longest of its kind to survive, its superiors having been demolished (Worksop Manor, Nottinghamshire) or remodelled (Longleat, Wiltshire). Over the years its original purpose has been variously diagnosed: in 1791 John Collinson described it as the original library, adding that 'the books and furniture were destroyed in the great rebellion'. J.P. Neale reiterated this in 1828, adding that it was 'afterwards converted into a picture gallery'. These statements are not supported by the inventories. In 1638 the gallery was sparsely furnished with four high chairs, twelve stools, four low stools and 'one mapp', and the room was evidently used by the family for recreation, especially in wet weather. In 1746 Edward Phelips celebrated his coming of age in this room, and during the early nineteenth century it was the setting for John Phelips's convivial evening entertainments.

It is possible that the Gallery originally had a tunnel vault ceiling with plasterwork decoration, but the survey of 1667 states simply that it was 'wainscoted'. The present quite plain ceiling, with its apologetic pendentives, dates from the time of John Phelips (1784–1834). It is not known when the original wainscoting disappeared, but in the nineteenth century plain pine panelling to dado height was installed, only to be stripped out in its turn, except at the north and south ends. Around the fireplaces, rising to cornice level, is older oak panelling. Five smaller rooms, occupying the wings of the house, lead off the Gallery. In 1638 these included four bedrooms, identified by their colour scheme: 'the primrose chamber', the 'blew bedd chamber', 'the wainscott chamber' and 'the white Chamber', resplendent with a 'silvered bedsted head and vallens of cloth of silver imbroidred and fringed with gold curtaines and quilt of white taffety'.

These rooms and the Gallery itself now contain a display of figures prominent in British history from Henry VIII to Charles I on loan from the National Portrait Gallery. The portraits are arranged in approximate chronological sequence.

On entering the Long Gallery turn left to Rooms 1 and 2.

These were originally one large room, but were converted into two rooms and a corridor, with consequent alterations to the simple plaster friezes and dados.

ROOM 1
The Reign of Henry VIII

Go to the west room at the end of the corridor and, beginning with the south wall, continue clockwise.

1 *Thomas Cromwell, Earl of Essex* (1485?–1540)
Statesman and right-hand-man of Wolsey. He suggested to Henry VIII that he make himself head of the Church of England to facilitate his divorce from Catherine of Aragon, and ruthlessly set about the dissolution of the monasteries. The failure of Henry's marriage to Anne of Cleves led to his downfall and execution.
After Hans Holbein (1497/8–1543), 1533–4.

2 *Henry VIII and the Tudor Dynasty*
An engraving after a copy of Hans Holbein's lost wall-painting in the Presence Chamber of the Palace of Whitehall, painted in 1537 and destroyed by fire in 1698. This shows Henry VII and his Queen, Elizabeth of York, and Henry VIII and his third Queen, Jane Seymour.
George Vertue (1683–1756), c.1737.

3 *Henry VIII* (1491–1547)
Reigned 1509–47. From Newburgh Priory, Yorkshire.
Unknown artist, c.1535–40.

4 *Edward VI* (1537–53)
Reigned 1547–53. The precocious and sickly son of Henry VIII by Jane Seymour, whose portrait hangs in the Crimson Bedroom. He was dominated first by the Duke of Somerset as Lord Protector, and later by the Duke of Northumberland, to whose daughter-in-law, Lady Jane Grey, he was induced to will the crown. Based on the drawing by Holbein at Windsor Castle.
After Hans Holbein (1497/8–1543), c.1542.

5 *Sir Thomas More* (1478–1535)
Wolsey's successor as Lord Chancellor (1529–32); the friend of Erasmus and patron of Holbein, a distinguished classical scholar and author of *Utopia* (1518); he opposed Henry VIII's divorce from Catherine of Aragon, and was executed for refusing to take the oath of supremacy; canonised 1935. The original of this portrait is in the Frick Collection, New York.
After Hans Holbein (1497/8–1543), 1527.

6 *Henry VIII* (1491–1547)
A version of the last portrait type of the King, of which the best example is at Castle Howard, Yorkshire.
Unknown artist, *c.*1542.

7 *Sir William Butts* (d.1545)
Physician to Henry and his court; a good early copy of the original in the Isabella Stewart Gardner Museum, Boston, where also is Holbein's portrait of Lady Butts.
After Hans Holbein (1497/8–1543), *c.*1540–3.

8 *Sir William Petre* (1505?–72)
Petre served Henry VIII, Edward VI, Mary I and Elizabeth I with equal fidelity as Secretary of State; at the Dissolution of the Monasteries he acquired enormous properties, owning 36,000 acres in Devonshire alone; he was granted a lease of the monastic lands at Montacute after the dissolution of the Priory in 1539. The Phelipses were sub-tenants of the Petres throughout the sixteenth century. Inscribed with the date 1567 and age 61.
Steven van der Meulen (fl.1543–68), 1567.

9 *Henry Howard, Earl of Surrey* (1517?–47)
Poet and soldier; son of the Duke of Norfolk, and companion of Henry VIII's illegitimate son, the Duke of Richmond; executed on a trumped-up charge of treason. He introduced blank verse to England, and, like Wyatt (10), experimented with Petrarchan verse forms.
After William Scrots (fl.1537–53), 1546.

10 *Sir Thomas Wyatt* (1503?–42)
Courtier and poet; a lover of Anne Boleyn before her marriage to Henry, and imprisoned for a time because of this; introduced the sonnet from Italy into England. He was the second holder of the former monastic lands at Montacute, and a close friend of Sir John Horsey of Clifton Maybank, where he died. He was buried in the Horsey tomb at Sherborne Abbey, and left his interest in Montacute to his mistress, Elizabeth Darrell.

(12) Thomas Wentworth, 2nd Baron Wentworth of Nettlestead; attributed to Steven van der Meulen, 1568

After a lost original by Hans Holbein (1497/8–1543), *c.*1540.

11 *Thomas Radcliffe, 3rd Earl of Sussex* (1526?–83)
Soldier and courtier, who served both Mary I and Elizabeth I as Lord Deputy of Ireland; as Lord President of the North he suppressed the rebellion of 1569. In this portrait he holds his white wand as Lord Chamberlain (1572), although the portrait-type originates *c.*1565.
Unknown artist, *c.*1572.

12 *Thomas Wentworth, 2nd Baron Wentworth of Nettlestead* (1525–84)
As Lord Deputy of Calais, 1553–8, he surrendered the port to the French in January 1558; acquitted of the charge of treasonable surrender, 1559. Inscribed with the date 1568 and the age 44. The jewel which hangs round his neck is inscribed 'FORTUN RU..', and his sword decorated with a figure of Fortune.
Attributed to Steven van der Meulen (fl.1543–68), 1568.

(15) Robert Sidney, 1st Earl of Leicester; by an unknown artist, c.1588

CORRIDOR (SOUTH WALL):

13 *Sir Richard Grenville* (1541?–91)
Naval commander and cousin of Sir Walter Ralegh (19), whom he helped in the colonisation of America; he converted Buckland Abbey in Devon from a Cistercian monastery into a private home, before selling it to Sir Francis Drake; mortally wounded on *The Revenge* off Flores in the Azores. His death was celebrated in Tennyson's famous ballad. Inscribed with the date 1571 and age 29.
After an unknown artist, 1571.

14 *Sir Christopher Hatton* (1540–91)
Statesman, who is said to have danced his way into Elizabeth I's favour; charged with being the Queen's lover by Mary, Queen of Scots (1584), he was a member of the committee which tried her (1586); Lord Chancellor, 1587–91; briefly held the grant of former monastic lands at Montacute after the death of Sir William Petre (8). In this portrait he holds a cameo of Elizabeth; the Latin motto means 'at length thus'.
Unknown artist, 1589.

15 *Robert Sidney, 1st Earl of Leicester* (1563–1626)
Soldier brother of Sir Philip Sidney; his life at Penshurst is described in a poem by Ben Jonson; created Earl of Leicester, 1618. The Latin motto signifies: 'I shall find a way or I shall make one', accompanied by an *impresa* of boughs bursting into flame. Leicester's armour is Milanese, and the gilt decoration of the shield represents Apollo as god of light. His baton probably alludes to his appointment as Governor of Flushing on 16 July 1588.
Unknown artist, *c.*1588.

Leading off the corridor on the north side is Room 2.

ROOM 2
Elizabeth I and her Court

16 *Sir Henry Sidney* (1529–86)
Father of Sir Philip and Robert Sidney (15), he was the ablest of the men who governed Ireland for Elizabeth, but his career was fatally entwined with that of his brother-in-law, Robert Dudley, Earl of Leicester (21). Inscribed with the date 1573 and age 44.
Unknown artist, 1573.

17 *Edward Fiennes de Clinton, 1st Earl of Lincoln* (1512–85)
Lord High Admiral (1550–4, 1558–85); a royal ward and attendant on Henry VIII, Lincoln first married Elizabeth Blount, the King's mistress and mother of his illegitimate son, Henry Fitzroy, Duke of Richmond. He survived the vicissitudes of four reigns in high office.
Unknown artist, 1584.

18 *Walter Devereux, 1st Earl of Essex* (1541?–76)
Irish adventurer, who undertook to conquer Ulster (1573), but was recalled after his useless and brutal raid on Rathlin; falsely rumoured to have been poisoned at the instigation of the Earl of Leicester (21), who married his widow, Lettice. Father of the 2nd Earl (20). The Latin motto signifies 'Envy is the companion of virtue'. Inscribed with the date 1572 and age 32.
Unknown artist, 1572.

19 *Sir Walter Ralegh* (1552?–1618)
Military and naval commander and author; a favourite of Elizabeth, but banished from court for his relationship with Elizabeth Throckmorton. He made his first voyage of discovery to the West Indies in 1578, and in 1584 established a short-lived settlement in America named Virginia. Imprisoned

(18) Walter Devereux, 1st Earl of Essex; by an unknown artist, 1572

for treason by James I (1603) – his former friend Sir Edward Phelips helped in the Crown prosecution; released in 1617, but finally executed. The damaged Latin motto signifies: 'by love and virtue', and is accompanied by a crescent moon, possibly in allusion to the Queen as Cynthia, goddess of the moon. Inscribed with the date 1588 and age 34.
Attributed to the monogrammist H (?Hubbard), 1588.

20 *Robert Devereux, 2nd Earl of Essex* (1566–1601)
Courtier and soldier; 'a man of nature not to be ruled', Essex captivated the Queen, but over-estimated the extent to which she would allow him to meddle in politics. His high-handed behaviour as Governor-General of Ireland (1599) led to his imprisonment; a long battle for power with Robert Cecil led to his futile attempt to raise a rebellion in London; executed for treason. The original of this portrait is the full-length at Woburn Abbey in Bedfordshire.
After Marcus Gheeraerts the Younger (1561/2–1636), *c.*1596.

21 *Robert Dudley, Earl of Leicester* (1532?–88)
Courtier and soldier; son of the Duke of Northumberland executed for championing Lady Jane Grey, Leicester narrowly escaped execution himself; Elizabeth's only serious English suitor, whose relationship with her lasted from her accession to his death; commander-in-chief of the unsuccessful expeditionary force to the Netherlands (1585) and of the army at Tilbury (1588), his career was marred by intrigue and scandal; briefly held the reversion of former monastic lands at Montacute (1574).
Unknown artist, *c.*1575–80.

22 *Elizabeth I* (1533–1603)
Reigned 1558–1603; the only child of Henry VIII and his second wife, Anne Boleyn. This is a version of the 'Armada' portrait of the Queen, of which the best-known version is at Woburn Abbey, commemorating the defeat of the Spanish Armada in 1588. It has evidently been cut down on all sides. Recent conservation revealed the original seascape background, which had been overpainted in dark green, presumably at the time the panel was reduced in size.
By or after George Gower (*c.*1540?–96), *c.*1588.

23 *Sir John Harington* (1561–1612)
Wit and author, and a godson of the Queen, who instructed him to translate Ariosto's *Orlando Furioso* (published 1591); banished from court on account of his satirical writings (1596); inventor of the water-closet.
Attributed to Hieronimo Custodis (fl.1589–95), *c.*1590–5.

24 *Sir Francis Walsingham* (1530–90)
Statesman and zealous Protestant; Secretary of State, 1573–90, employed in foreign affairs; from 1596 was chief of the secret service in London; advocated intervention in the Low Countries, and the elimination of Mary, Queen of Scots.
After John de Critz the Elder (*c.*1552–1642), *c.*1585.

25 *William Cecil, 1st Baron Burghley* (1520–98)
Elizabeth's principal adviser and most diligent minister for forty years; appointed Secretary of State in 1558, and Lord High Treasurer from 1572. Portrayed here with his white wand as Lord High Treasurer, and wearing, unusually, the great collar of the Garter without the Great George, but with the Lesser George on a double gold chain.
Unknown artist, after 1572.

(22) Elizabeth I; by or after George Gower, c.1588

FURNITURE

Two carved oak cupboards, perhaps nineteenth century.

Return to the Long Gallery and cross over to Room 3.

ROOM 3
The Elizabethan Age

26 *William Shakespeare* (1564–1616)
A later impression (1632 or after) of the engraved frontispiece from the *First Folio* edition of Shakespeare's plays, published in 1623.
Martin Droeshout (1601–50?), 1623.

27 *Sir Nicholas Bacon* (1509–79)
Lord Keeper of the Great Seal (1558), and an outspoken opponent of Mary, Queen of Scots; father of Sir Francis Bacon (56). Inscribed with the date 1579, age 68, and the Bacon family motto, *Mediocria firma*, 'mediocrity is safe'. He is portrayed with his seal bag as Lord Keeper.
Unknown artist, 1579.

28 *Thomas Sackville, 1st Earl of Dorset* (1536–1608)
Poet, playwright, statesman and owner of Knole; co-author of *Gorboduc*, the first English tragedy in blank verse, described by Vita Sackville-West as 'of unbearable dullness'; as commissioner at state trials, he announced to Mary, Queen of Scots her sentence of death. Inscribed with the date 1601 and age 63.
Attributed to John de Critz the Elder (*c*.1552–1642), 1601.

29 *Elizabeth Talbot, Countess of Shrewsbury* (1518–1608)
'Bess of Hardwick'; four times married, and one of the greatest landowners of the day; the builder of Hardwick Hall, the first house at Chatsworth, and many others. The original of this portrait is at Hardwick.
After an unknown artist, *c*.1590.

30 *Sir Edmund Anderson* (1530–1605)
Judge; took part in the trials of Mary, Queen of Scots, Essex (20) and Ralegh (19); showed great severity to Puritans.
Unknown artist, *c*.1590–1600.

31 *Sir Thomas Chaloner the Elder* (1521–65)
Diplomat and Latin versifier. Dated 1559, this portrait was probably painted in the Low Countries where Chaloner was on a diplomatic mission in that year. Its emblematic theme is presumably of the sitter's devising. The Latin inscription (top right) describes the realisation by King Sardanapalus, King of Assyria, that all mortal things perish: 'they fade black and begrimed with soot as though gold were nothing else but smoke; but the mind increases with cultivation and, after death, becomes even clearer; the power is in the mind. Remaining vanities flee.' Chaloner holds a pair of balances in which a book, encircled by a halo of light, outweighs a winged globe and gold and jewels.
Unknown Flemish artist, 1559.

32 *Sir Edward Rogers* (1498?–1567?)
Esquire of the body to Henry VIII; Elizabeth's Comptroller of the Household, 1560–5; with his white wand as Comptroller. Inscribed with the date 1567 and age 69.
Unknown artist, 1567.

33 *Sir Thomas Coningsby* (1551–1625)
This young soldier is portrayed with the accoutrements of falconry: he holds the falcon's hood in one hand, and with the other swings the lure, while in the sky above flies the falcon itself. The fragmentary Latin and Italian inscriptions suggest an allegory in which the falcon symbolises youth and indiscipline, and the falconer maturity and control.
Attributed to George Gower (*c*.1540?–96), 1572.

34 *Sir Richard Bingham* (1528–99)
Soldier and Governor of Connaught, 1584; imprisoned on a charge of exercising undue severity in 1596, he nevertheless returned to Ireland as Marshal in 1598.
Unknown artist, 1564.

35 *Sir Nicholas Throckmorton* (1515–71)
Diplomat; on Elizabeth's accession appointed Chief Butler, Chamberlain of the Exchequer, and Ambassador to France, 1560; throughout his career much involved in negotiations with Mary, Queen of Scots; imprisoned on the suspicion of being sympathetic to the Northern Rebellion, 1569.
Unknown, probably French, artist, *c*.1562.

36 *Elizabeth I* (1533–1603)
Reigned 1558–1603. An especially stylised and hierarchical portrait, using a face-mask of the Queen which originated with the so-called 'Darnley' portrait in the NPG.
Unknown artist, *c*.1585–90.

37 *Edward de Vere, 17th Earl of Oxford* (1550–1604)
Courtier and son-in-law of Burghley (25). His violent temper led him to quarrel with Sir Philip

(35) Sir Nicholas Throckmorton; by an unknown, probably French, artist, c.1562

Sidney, and to disgrace at court, 1582–3; one of the judges of Mary, Queen of Scots. After an original of 1575. (On loan from a private collection.)
Unknown artist.

38 *Richard Bancroft* (1544–1610)
Bishop of London, 1597, and Archbishop of Canterbury, 1604–10; he defended the rights of ecclesiastical courts and was a vehement opponent of Puritanism.
Unknown artist, after 1604.

39 *Sir Thomas Fleming* (1544–1613)
Judge who served as Solicitor-General, 1595, Chief-Baron of the Exchequer, 1604, Chief-Justice of the King's Bench, 1607, and who tried the gunpowder plotters. Inscribed with the date 1596 and age 51.
Unknown artist, 1596.

40 *William Camden* (1551–1623)
Antiquary and historian; appointed headmaster of Westminster School, 1593; published the first edition of his *Britannia*, 1586. Montacute is mentioned for the first time in the 1607 edition. The Latin motto signifies: 'in weight, not in number', and the portrait is inscribed with the date 1609 and age 58.

After Marcus Gheeraerts the Younger (1561/2–1636), 1609.

Return to the Long Gallery, starting to north of the entrance door.

WEST WALL:

41 *James I of England and VI of Scotland* (1566–1625)
Reigned in Scotland from 1567, and England 1603–25. Inscribed with the age 8 and date 1574.
Attributed to Rowland Lockey (c.1565–1616) after Arnold van Brounckhorst (fl.1566–80), 1574.

42 *John Thornborough* (1551–1641)
Chaplain to Elizabeth I; Bishop of Worcester, 1617–41; especially zealous against recusants; wrote works supporting union with Scotland. Inscribed with the date 1630 and age 80.
Unknown artist, 1630.

43 *Charles Howard, 1st Earl of Nottingham* (1536–1624)
Lord High Admiral, 1585–1618, and, as Lord Howard of Effingham, commander-in-chief against the Spanish Armada, 1588. Wearing Garter robes.
After an unknown artist, c.1602.

44 *William Cecil, 1st Baron Burghley* (1520–98)
Lord High Treasurer, 1572–98, chief minister and trusted adviser of Elizabeth I. Holding his wand as Lord High Treasurer.
Unknown artist, 1590s.

EAST WALL:

45 *James Hay, 1st Earl of Carlisle* (d.1636)
Courtier noted for his splendid hospitality; a favourite of both James I and Charles I.
Unknown artist, 1628.

46 *Henry Wriothesley, 3rd Earl of Southampton* (1573–1624)
Favourite of Elizabeth I and patron of Shakespeare; his tempestuous relationship with the Queen culminated in involvement in Essex's rebellion; his death sentence was commuted to life imprisonment; freed by James I and reinstated. His superb armour, now in the Tower Armouries, is French, and was probably purchased by Southampton on a diplomatic mission to France in 1598. (On loan from a private collection.)
Unknown artist, c.1600.

47 *Lodovic Stuart, 2nd Duke of Lennox and 1st Duke of Richmond* (1574–1624)
Courtier; next in succession to the Scottish throne

after James VI; Lord High Admiral of Scotland, 1591; after James's accession to the English throne, Steward of the Household; wearing Garter robes and holding his white wand as Steward.
Attributed to Paul van Somer (c.1577/8–1622), c.1620.

WINDOW BAY:

48 *William I, 'The Conqueror'* (1027–87)
Reigned 1066–87.

49 *Henry I* (1068–1135)
Reigned 1100–35.

50 *Stephen* (1097?–1154)
Reigned 1135–54.

51 *Henry II* (1133–89)
Reigned 1154–89.

52 *John* (1167?–1216)
Reigned 1199–1216.

53 *Henry III* (1207–72)
Reigned 1216–72.

54 *Edward III* (1312–77)
Reigned 1327–77.

55 *Richard II* (1367–1400)
Reigned 1377–99.

From a set of portraits of early kings and queens of England, formerly in the collection of the Dukes of Leeds at Hornby Castle, Yorkshire. The rest of the set is in the window bay opposite. Hieratic in style and richly gilded, they are probably by more than one artist.
Unknown artist, or artists, sixteenth century.

56 *Francis Bacon, Viscount St Albans* (1561–1626)
Lawyer, natural philosopher and essayist; Lord Chancellor 1618–21, when he was charged with bribery and confessed that he was guilty of 'corruption and neglect'. Sir Robert Phelips was chairman of the committee of enquiry into the charges. Published *The Advancement of Learning* (1605) and *Essays* (1625). Died of a chill caught stuffing a fowl with snow, to test the preservation of flesh by freezing.
Unknown artist, after 1731, after an original of c.1620.

57 *Sir Thomas Edmondes* (1563?–1639)
Diplomat and MP; known as the 'little man' on account of his diminutive stature, he is portrayed with his white wand as Treasurer of the Household under James I.
Daniel Mytens (c.1590–1647), c.1620.

(46) Henry Wriothesley, 3rd Earl of Southampton; by an unknown artist, c.1600

58 *Philip Herbert, 4th Earl of Pembroke* (1584–1650)
Courtier, favourite of James I and Lord Chamberlain, 1626–41; with his brother, the 3rd Earl, one of the 'incomparable paire of brethren' to whom the *First Folio* of Shakespeare is dedicated (1623); patron of Van Dyck, and rebuilder of Wilton House in Wiltshire. He is portrayed in Garter robes.
Unknown artist, c.1615.

WEST WALL:

59 *Charles I* (1600–49)
Reigned 1625–49; shown here when Prince of Wales. This portrait was formerly in the collection of the Dukes of Marlborough at Blenheim Palace, but may well be the portrait by the Flemish artist Blyenberch which the King himself owned. The

(80) Sir Edward Hoby; by an unknown artist, 1583

the 3rd Earl of Southampton (46), much to the Queen's displeasure, in 1598: 'some say she hath taken a venew under the girdle and swells upon it, yet she complaines not of fowle play, but says the Erle of Southampton will justifie it'.
Unknown artist, c.1620.

82 *James I of England and VI of Scotland* (1566–1625)
Reigned in Scotland from 1567, England 1603–25.
After John de Critz the Elder (c.1552–1642), 1606.

83 *James I (1566–1625) and Henry Frederick, Prince of Wales (1594–1612)*
Engraving, altered from a plate of 1621 showing the King and Charles I as Prince of Wales, to serve as a memorial print to James I (d.1625) and Henry, Prince of Wales. Despite the change of identity, no alteration is made to the Prince's physiognomy in the revised state; only the caption changes, and skulls replace James's orb and a hat held in the Prince's left hand.
Willem de Passe (1590–c.1660), 1621; altered 1625.

84 *George Villiers, 1st Duke of Buckingham* (1592–1628) *and his Family*
The Duke is seen with his wife, Katherine Manners (d.1649) and his children, Mary (1622–85), later Lady Herbert and Duchess of Richmond, and George (1628–87), later 2nd Duke. The original of this group (Royal Collection) must have been painted between spring 1628, when the Dutch artist Honthorst first came to England, and August of the same year, when the Duke, the unpopular favourite of James I and Charles I, was assassinated at Portsmouth. He was the political patron of Sir Robert Phelips.
After Gerrit van Honthorst (1590–1656), 1628.

85 *Elizabeth, Queen of Bohemia (1596–1662)*
'The Winter Queen'; the eldest daughter of James I, she married in 1613 Frederick, Elector Palatine, one of the leaders of the Protestants in Germany. Sir Edward Phelips, the builder of Montacute, organised the Masque of the Middle Temple, which formed part of their wedding celebrations. George Chapman's script contained lavish praise of the Virginia Company, of which Sir Edward and his son Richard were both prominent members. In 1619 Frederick accepted the crown of Bohemia, but the couple's expulsion from Bohemia a year later sparked off the Thirty Years War.
Studio of Michiel Jansz. van Miereveldt (1567–1641), c.1623.

FURNITURE

A cypress wood chest decorated with penwork, Venetian, late sixteenth century.

Return to the Long Gallery and cross over to Room 5.

ROOM 5
The Jacobean Age

86 *John Fletcher (1579–1625)*
Prolific dramatist, who collaborated on many plays with Francis Beaumont, including *The Maid's Tragedy* (1611) and *Philaster* (1610); also worked with Massinger and Shakespeare.
After an unknown artist, ?late seventeenth century.

87 *Ben Jonson (1573?–1637)*
Dramatist and poet, best known for his satirical comedies *Every Man in his Humour* (in which Shakespeare acted), *Volpone* and *The Alchemist*.
After Abraham van Blyenberch (fl.1617–22), c.1617.

Marty 12
Anno Domini
1614

No Spring Till now.

(91) Mary Throckmorton, Lady Scudamore; by Marcus Gheeraerts the Younger, 1615

CHAPTER EIGHT
THE GARDEN, PARK AND ESTATE

Long before Montacute House was built, there was a park in the area, created before the end of the eleventh century by the Counts of Mortain and granted in 1192 to the Cluniac Priory which they had founded. Lying some 200 yards to the south west of the present park, and known later as the Old Park, it was essentially an enclosure for deer. After the dissolution of the Priory in 1539 it presumably fell into agricultural use, and today this area is merely two fields of pasture divided by a small scrubby stream-valley and enclosed on three sides by a woodland belt called Park Covert, but its topography – a steep natural amphitheatre – makes

One of the mixed flower and shrub borders to the east court. The planting was devised by Phyllis Reiss of nearby Tintinhull

the nearby, more rolling, Montacute Park, seem dull by comparison.

In the 1590s Edward Phelips began building his great house at Montacute, and a new park was presumably created at about the same time. Nothing is known for certain about its layout or area, although it most probably included some of the present park, and perhaps an avenue on the line of the present Lime Avenue. In 1608 Phelips bought the land of the former Priory, but whether he incorporated any of this, which included the Old Park, into the new is not known. Ridge and furrow covers much of the park today, indicating that it was once arable land, probably part of the common fields of Montacute village, and it may well have been built up piecemeal by Phelips as he was able to acquire more land.

It is probable also that the garden was created around the time of the building of the house. Its layout, with enclosed courtyard entrance, raised walks, axial, symmetrical pattern, relating directly to the form of the house, is typical of the period. In 1630 Gerard described the house as having 'large and spacious Courtes, gardens, orchards, a parke', but the first detailed information on the garden at Montacute comes in a survey of 1667, and it is worth quoting this in full:

Out of the Porch of the house Eastward there is a descent of 4 Stepps into a large Tarris [terrace] walke paved with Freestone and Rayles and Ballasters with very large high Pillers of Freestone and Piramids betweene, all of Freestone from which Tarris walke there is a descent of 6 Stepps into a faire Court with a Freestone walke in the midst leading to a Gatehouse which Court is walled about with Freestone Ashler Wall topped with Rayles and Ballesters and Piramids and Turrets of Ornament, in the middle of the East Wall part of the said Court is a faire Gatehouse with lodging Chambers of Freestone and at each corner of the said Court are 2 faire Turretts with lodging Chambers, all built with Freestone.

Without the Gatehouse is another faire large Court walled about and coped with Freestone sett with Severall walkes and Rowes of Trees, on the North side of Which Court is a faire Bowling Greene sett about with goodly rowes of Trees, and variety of pleasant walkes Arbours and Coppices full of delight and pleasure.

On the North side of the house is a very faire Spacious Garden walled about and furnished with all sorts of Flowers and fruits and divers mounted walkes without which Garden there is a descent of about 10 stepps into Private walkes walled about and furnished with store of fruite, and at the end of the East walke there is a faire Banqueting house built and Arched with Freestone wainscoted within and leaded on the Toppe thereof, and without the West Walke of the Garden there is a faire Orchard furnished with good fruit and divers pleasant Walkes.

On the South side of the house there is a large Woodyard and necessary buildings for Daryes Washing Brewing and Bakeing, a Pigeon house, and on the South side thereof, and of the Courts before the house, are severall Orchards of Cherryes, Pares, Plumbs, others of Apples, and also good Kitchen gardens with 2 fish pounds all incompassed within a wall.

On the West side of the house there is a large Voyd Court Sett with Rowes of Trees in order, of Elmes and Walnutts leading to the Stables Barnes Stawles and other large buildings for servants Granaryes and other necessary uses where are also severall Fish ponds and also a hopp garden of an Acre and a halfe.

All this containes 24 Acres or thereabouts and is Valued at 4000 li.

This probably describes the grounds more or less as originally laid out, and much of this outline – the north garden, the east court, and the kitchen garden – survives today.

A particularly interesting feature of the north garden was the 'Banqueting house'. In the late sixteenth century many such small rooms were built, either roof turrets as at Longleat and Hardwick or separate buildings as at Montacute, where the host and his guests would retire after dinner for a final course of 'banquet' delicacies – crystallised quince paste, ginger bread and other such sweet items.

Between 1667 and 1750, when Edward Phelips (1725–97) took over the estate, little changed. Disputed inheritance had led to years of neglect, and he found an estate burdened with debt, and probably depleted of much of its best timber (there was a sale to the navy in 1728). Some outlying lands had to

be sold off, but gradually Montacute was revived. A Latin inscription in the east window of the Library, which was almost certainly inscribed by Edward Phelips, suggests that he was a practical man with a love of growing things: 'happy too is the man who cares for his fields; who appreciates all the manifold riches of his garden; who has learnt the art of grafting trees; who knows which particular plants thrive in which soil . . .' Edward's diary and autobiography also reveal that he was involved in the day-to-day running of his house and estate, and other fragmentary details of life at Montacute emerge. In 1778, for instance, he records putting out the orange trees (implying there was perhaps an orangery for overwintering the trees); the bowling green mentioned in 1667 was still in use – he played bowls (and fives) at Montacute in 1771; in 1760 the folly tower was built on St Michael's Hill. The first detailed map of Montacute, made in Phelips's time by Samuel Donne (c.1782), shows the house and grounds largely as in the seventeenth century, though some changes have been made – the banqueting house and gatehouse have disappeared completely; a mount and pond are shown in the north garden, and the axial double avenue, now the Lime Avenue, is shown for the first time, as is the tower on St Michael's Hill with its winding approach and bower of trees; there is a bridge in the middle of the avenue, with ponds marked nearby.

J. Bonnor's view of the east front of Montacute, commissioned by Phelips in 1784 for Collinson's *History of Somerset*, gives more information, though allowance has to be made for artistic licence. Only one side of the double avenue is shown, giving a wider panorama, and some details are inaccurate – the Dutch gables of the house are drawn straight. A long serpentine pool, however, is shown in the park, crossed by a stone bridge with a balustrade with finials identical to those of the wall of the east court. At the southern end of the pool is a rustic stone grotto with a statue of a female nude. The eastern wall of the east court is depicted more as a fence than a stone wall, with no central gateway, and with a stone pillar nearby. Indeed, the materials for the bridge probably came from the wall of the east court, or from the far east court, which had been demolished by this date. The tower on St

Engraving of the east front of Montacute by J. Bonner, from Collinson's 'History of Somerset' (1784)

Michael's Hill is shown, flying a huge flag, and the whole vista is framed by gnarled oak trees. How much of this is accurate is uncertain – maps record the bridge and pool, but the grotto is not documented elsewhere.

Until the 1780s the main entrance to the house was on the east front, approached through the east court, from the main road to Ilchester, which ran at right angles to the front of the house. All this changed, however, around 1785 when Phelips began to build his new west front to the house and a drive leading to it. He records:

1785

On the 19th of December I began forming a New Road to the West Front of Montacute house from the publick Road thro Boys Court Orchard by Filling up millponds Levelling Hedges and c. And in the Course of the Xmas I began Digging the foundation for the New West Front which were very great and Arduous Undertakings at My advanced season of life.

1787

This year was remarkable for . . . making an Entire new road to [the West Front] thro Boys Court by filling up two large mill ponds and levelling much ground.

The new west drive wound gently from a lodge on the road at the west to a turning circle in front of the west front. The house was screened from the road by a wooded belt; the stable block, which had formed the western boundary of the 'large Voyd Court' or basecourt of 1667 must have been demolished just prior to the building of the new drive, along with the mill. Once the west drive had been constructed, the east court could be turned into a garden, although it is not known to be definitely such until 1812, in the time of John Phelips, when a watercolour by John Buckler shows it laid out as today, although with stone-flagged, rather than gravel, paths.

The Montacute parish map of 1825 is quite detailed and shows the serpentine west drive with its lodge, the pool with bridge or causeway, and several new buildings in the north garden. The pond and mount are gone; a small building appears on the site of the present orangery, and the Yew Walk (Fig Walk) is also shown, with a building at its southern end, possibly the prototype of the present summer-house. Most of the northern part of the park is pasture, but the majority of the southern part is still arable or arable strips. In 1830 two views of the house by J. P. Neale show fan-trained pear trees growing against the west front (the last of these was removed in 1967), and the east terrace softened with climbing plants on the pillars and with large pots of plants.

After John Phelips's death in 1834, the house was let. In 1835 Harriet and Charlotte Grove of Coker Court visited, and Charlotte noted in her diary, 'It is uninhabited and looks very desolate. The flower garden is all overgrown.' Ten years later, William Phelips married Ellen Helyar of Coker Court (the daughter of Harriet Grove) and moved into Montacute. Ellen brought with her the gardener, Mr Pridham, and together they designed a new garden. Some of their plans survive. One shows the pro-

posed layout of the north garden, with parterres with an intricate arrangement of beds, laid out on a quartered square pattern with a central fountain, recreating the flavour of a Tudor garden, and enclosed by the existing terrace walks. An undated early photograph proves that this plan was executed, although the fountain has a balustrade and a different central feature. The Orangery is shown in a sketch entitled 'new Garden Green House' of 1848. Pridham and Ellen Phelips were also responsible for the present west drive (1851–2) which runs straight to the house and is flanked by avenues of yews, cedars and Wellingtonias. At about the same time (before 1855) the public road was rerouted further west, giving the new drive extra length, and making the old lodge obsolete. In 1853 the railway was built, and became the northern boundary of the park, screened by belts of trees. To the south east much of the arable land was converted to park, and planted with mixed clumps and circles of trees and a belt of woodland. The east court was again remodelled about this time. The eastern wall was put back in its original position linking the two pav-

A detail of the Montacute parish map of 1825, which shows the late eighteenth-century west drive winding through Boys Court to the main road

The Montacute
stables in 1840.
This range was
rebuilt following the
construction of the
west drive, but has
now gone; drawing by
John Buckler (British
Library)

The borders of the east court, painted by George Samuel Elgood in 1886 (Christopher Wood Gallery)

ilions, flower beds created, Irish Yews planted and a fountain basin installed as the central feature.

The Cedar Lawn (then called the bowling green), which is shown with several trees in 1885, was enclosed, and some of the eighteenth-century features of the park – the pool and the bridge – removed. The grotto had perhaps gone in John Phelips's time. Almost all these alterations were sympathetic to the character of Montacute, and seem to have been deliberate attempts to restore the essence of the original layout, albeit with a Victorian flavour.

During the late nineteenth and early twentieth centuries the Montacute estate was impoverished. Land was sold off piecemeal, and it seems unlikely that any further major alterations were made, although Mrs Ingilby notes a garden made by her mother (W. R. Phelips's wife) before her death in 1877, beyond the Column Garden. In 1893 a watercolour by E. A. Rowe shows the complexities of the north garden parterre reduced to four meagre central oval beds; these disappeared in their turn c.1900–1.

THE GARDENS TODAY

THE KITCHEN GARDEN

Visitors today park their cars in what was until 1971 the walled kitchen garden of Montacute. Now fallen from favour for economic reasons, such gardens were once a vital part of the life of a country house, supplying fresh fruit and vegetables for the many people who lived there. Fruit trees were trained against the walls: nectarines and figs on the south-facing wall; pears, plums and apples, the west. There were peach and vine houses; melon and cucumber frames; strawberry and asparagus beds, as well as more common vegetables, fruit and herbs, and several beehives. Now the garden is laid to lawn, and spaciously planted with Norway maples and limes. A second kitchen garden to the south contains the overflow car-park and plant sales.

A door in the wall to the right of the shop leads to the Cedar Lawn.

THE CEDAR LAWN

This extensive lawn with a pair of tall cedars at its south end was formerly known, according to the manorial survey map of c.1782, as Pig's Wheatie Orchard, and was converted into a bowling green in the nineteenth century. The wall on the west side supports fan-trained fig trees (planted by the Trust c.1945) and the servants' path which runs its length is screened from the rest of the garden by a clipped yew hedge. At the south end is the probably nineteenth-century arcaded garden house, with an Elizabethan façade sometimes said to have been added by Lord Curzon, but perhaps imported earlier. This has in its heraldic achievement the arms of the Strode family, and it seems likely that it was removed from nearby Barrington Court, the Strode family home. Behind it rise up two specimens of *Cupressus arizonica*, the tallest English examples of this tender cypress. To the east lies the Column Garden, flanked on the north side by four Doric columns and bordered by clipped yews, featuring two large beds of *Yucca recurvifolia*. Beyond is a small orchard. Pairs of clipped yews march along the east side of the lawn, and at the north end are two shady sweet chestnuts, *Castanea sativa*. The white-painted garden seats were made to a design by the architect Sir Edwin Lutyens. In the north-east corner, by the east court pavilion, a gate leads into the park. There is a fine view of the house from the Lime Avenue.

Crossing the walk which leads to the south-east pavilion, enter the east court.

THE EAST COURT

This is bounded on three sides by balustraded walls of Ham stone, adorned with lanterns and obelisks; and, on the west, by the terrace of the house. The old walls shelter mixed flower and shrub borders, which have recently been replanted following the colour scheme devised in the 1950s by Mrs Phyllis Reiss of nearby Tintinhull. Strong clear colours and large groups of foliage plants provide interest throughout the year and are a bold and effective foil to the rich Ham stone of the house. The main

The north garden

features of the borders are the clematis and vines on the north and south walls; red 'Frensham' roses, 'Orange Triumph' polyantha roses, blue delphiniums and yellow lupins, dahlias and *Achillea*, and the dark foliage of *Berberis* and *Cotinus*. The spiny *Acanthus* and *Yucca*, the feathery fronds of *Macleaya*, and *Crambe maritima*, with its snow-storm of honey-scented flowers, add architectural interest. The fountain at the centre of the court was removed by Curzon, and the area turfed over around 1948 by the Trust. There is a fine *Magnolia grandiflora* against the north-east corner of the house.

A gate near the north-west corner leads to the broad raised walk which leads to the north-east pavilion, and then to the north garden.

THE NORTH GARDEN

This is bounded by raised walks, and, on west and north sides, by hedges of yew. Within these are rows of clipped Irish yews flanked by trees of a hybrid American thorn, *Crataegus × lavallei*, which make round heads in contrast to the erect yews. Below the raised walk on the south side is a border of shrub roses containing several ancient varieties which were in cultivation when the house was built: notably *Rosa gallica officinalis*, the red rose of Lancaster, and its 'sport', *Rosa gallica 'Versicolor'* ('Rosa Mundi'), and the double white form of the Yorkist rose, *Rosa alba* 'Maxima'. There are large bushes of the Chinese *Rosa moyesii*, a yellow hybrid of the Scotch or Burnet Rose, *Rosa pimpinellifolia lutea*, the climbing form of 'Souvenir de la Malmaison', named in honour of the Empress Josephine, and several hybrid musks and forms of *Rosa rugosa*, a Japanese species. The roses are underplanted with *Hosta fortunei hyacinthina*, in a plan devised by Graham Thomas from an idea by Vita Sackville-West, *c*.1945. At the centre is a pond and balustrade, part of work recorded in the 1890s by R. S. Balfour and by Reginald Blomfield. From the raised walk on the north side are good views over the park, and a gap in the yew hedge at the northwest corner gives access to the steps and path which lead down to the ice house, sunk in the north wall and brick-lined. Above the portal is a Latin inscription signifying: 'Freshness springs from ice and snow'. At the west end of the raised walk on the south side is the Orangery, built in 1848. It is a cold house containing specimens of *Jasminum polyanthum*, a tender honeysuckle, standard lippias (aloysias) and fuschias, and tuberous begonias during the summer months, as well as palms. Tubs of *Agapanthus* stand outside in the summer.

From the Orangery a path leads round to the west front of the house and the west drive.

THE WEST DRIVE

Here an avenue of clipped Irish Yew, Lebanon Cedars, beeches, limes and oaks leads down to the west gates, the gate-piers topped with the Phelips family crest (baskets of flames), and bearing the date 1787. Its future is ensured by a planting of young limes behind. There is a superb view of the west front from the gates. The west door of the house is flanked by emphatic banks of clipped box and *Choiysa ternata*. The south drive leads back in the direction of the car-park. It is fringed with large, feathery bushes, the remnants of huge Californian Redwoods planted by William and Ellen Phelips, and cut down during the Second World War. Opposite flourishes a Monterey (Californian) Cypress of record size, *Cupressus macrocarpa*. By the stable block are wide-spreading golden yews, *Taxus baccata aurea*.

THE PARK

In 1978 a replanting scheme for the park was devised, based on historical research, and since then there has been much replanting, both of individual specimen trees and also of oaks in the Oak Avenue, which runs south-east from the Lime Avenue. The severe gales of recent years have sadly depleted the mature trees. The Odcombe Lodge stands on the Odcombe road. Walks can be taken in the park and a leaflet detailing these and others in the neighbourhood, including that to the folly tower on St Michael's Hill, is on sale in the Trust shop.

THE CHURCH

The north transept of the parish church of St Catherine in Montacute village contains monuments to the Phelips family, including four recumbent effigies. The earliest is claimed (according to the inscription) to represent David Phelips (d.1484). Two are unidentified and the fourth, which is surmounted by a canopy, has effigies of Thomas Phelips (*c*.1500–89/90) and his wife. A classical wall monument commemorates Sir Edward Phelips (1638–99) and his wife, Edith (1662–1728).

Plan of the Estate, *c.*1782

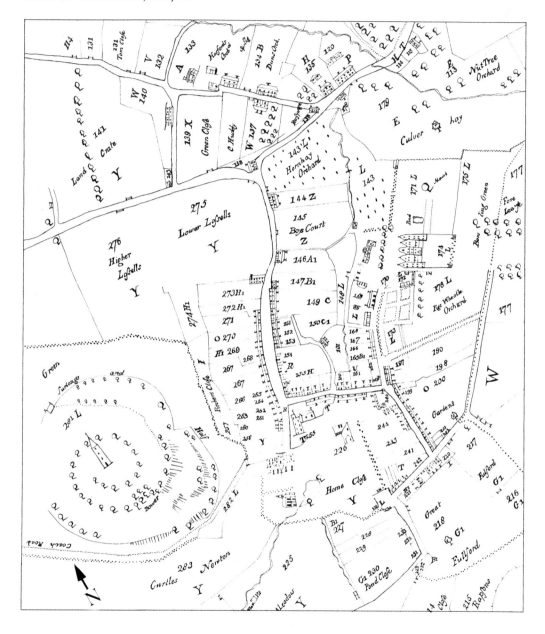

KEY

L means 'Edward Phelips Esq. In hand.'

143 Hornhay orchard

148 Redstreake orchard, ponds, mill and mill road

162, 163, 165 B1, 166, 167, 168 } houses and cottages

169 Barns, stalls, bartons, kennel, granary

170 Coach house, stables, hay barton, stable yard, etc.

171 Best garden, terrace walks, pond, etc.

172 Wood barton, dairyhouse, brewhouse, etc.

173 Kitchen garden.

174 Mansion house and forecourt

175 Outer bowling green

1638

THE DININGE ROOME

8 peice of arras hanginges

1 fine arras carpet with armes...

2 turkie carpettes

1 greene high velvet chaire

2 low stooles fringed with gold & silke

2 low chaires laced with broad gold lace sutable to them

2 high chaires 4 low stooles & 12 high stooles of new greene velvet, 2 arminge chaires, 2 high chaires without armes, 4 low stooles & 12 high stooles of old greene velvet

3 longe cushions laced with gold lace

2 green serge curtaines

4 curtaine rods,

16 pictures,

1 longe table bord

2 sidebords

1 pre [pair] of tables

a pre of great brass andirons

a pre of creeps [?Creepers, small intermediate andirons]

1728

GREAT DINING ROOM

a long Table board

Two Chests

Eight Crimson Stools

two Elbow Chairs

Eight Velvett Stools

a Two Elbow Chair

purple Sattin Chair embroidered with Gold and three Stools of the same

One Octagon Table

two Tea Tables

Pictures

Sir Robt Phelipps

Master of the Rolls

Marchioness of Northampton

Councellor Phelipps

Mad^m Edith Phelipps

Coll. Phelipps

Sundry boxes and a Trunk not looked into

A Quantity of Dry Elm board

A quantity of Wallnut plank & severall other Lumber Goods

1834

LIBRARY

Entailed property

3 Tables

2 Arm chairs

Books

China

2 Stools

2 Pictures

Sale Catalogue

Mahogany Library chair with steps complete

Eight carved oak chairs and two ditto with arms, covered with crimson damask

Oak sofa with three cushions ditto ditto

One ditto ditto ditto

Pair foot stools ditto ditto

Pair stools with loose covers

Pair ditto ditto larger

A squab with a silk cover

Fine toned grand pianoforte, by *Broadwood and Sons*

Double acting pedal harp with gold mountings

Mahogany canterbury

Small oak table

Oak stand for flowers

Two small octagon tables

Lady's work table

Painted tea magazine

Small mahogany table

Two black stands

Two fire screens

Handsome stand with foreign marble slab

Ditto ditto British ditto

Set of yew tree bookshelves

Theodolite on a mahogany stand, complete

Oak library table covered with crimson cloth, and a set of shelves on ditto

Large ditto ditto with ten drawers, covered with blue cloth

Large oak table covered with crimson cloth on handsome carved legs

Pair of 18 inch globes in oak frames

Two large oak inkstands with glasses

Two oak letter boxes

Painted box with musical glasses

Bronze stand with an almanack

Ditto taper, phosphoric match case, and marble weight

Three English china flower pots

Three ditto ditto

Handsome Brussels carpet, about 42 feet long by 19½ broad, with four pieces for recesses

Hearth rug

Worked ottoman

Mahogany reading stand

Two tambour frames

Seven linen roller blinds

Four white plaster busts

Three ditto children

Two black busts.

BIBLIOGRAPHY

MONTACUTE

BLOMFIELD, Reginald, *The Formal Garden in England*, London, 1892.

BROWN, Jane, *The Art and Architecture of English Gardens*, London, 1989, pp.124–5, 128–9.

COLLINSON, Rev. John, *History and Antiquities of the County of Somerset* (3 vols) 1791.

CORNFORTH, John, 'The Significance of Montacute, 1931–81', *Country Life*, 26 November 1981.

CORYATE, Thomas, *Crudities. Hastily gobled up in Five Months Travells*, 1611.

COUNTRY LIFE, 12 and 19 June 1915; 20, 27 October and 3 November 1955 (by Arthur Oswald).

FRETWELL, K.A., *Montacute: Park and Garden Survey*, 1988.

GLYN, Sir Anthony, *Elinor Glyn*, London, 1955.

LINES, Charles, *Montacute and the Phelips Family*, n.d.

OSWALD, Arthur, *Country Houses of Dorset*, London, 1959.

PEVSNER, Sir Nikolaus, *The Buildings of England: South & West Somerset*, London, 1958.

PHELIPS, J.H.C., 'Phelips of Montacute: Two Early Representatives', *Somerset and Dorset Notes and Queries*, xxxi, Part 313, March 1981.

POWYS, Llewelyn, *Somerset Essays*, London, 1937.

ROSE, Kenneth, *Superior Person: a portrait of Curzon and his circle in late Victorian England*, London, 1969.

VICTORIA COUNTY HISTORY, The County of Somerset, iii, London, 1974.

WELLS-COLE, Anthony, 'An oak bed at Montacute', *Furniture History*, xvii, 1981.

TUDOR AND JACOBEAN PORTRAITURE

MILLAR, Oliver, *The Age of Charles I*, Tate Gallery, 1972.

PIPER, David, *The English Face*, London, 1957.

PIPER, David, *National Portrait Gallery: Seventeenth Century Portraits*, London, 1963.

STRONG, Roy, *National Portrait Gallery: Tudor and Jacobean Portraits*, London, 1969.

STRONG, Roy, *The English Icon*, London, 1969.

STRONG, Roy, *The Elizabethan Image*, Tate Gallery, 1969.

TAPESTRY

HEINZ, D., *Medieval Tapestries*, London, 1967.

THOMSON, W.G., *A History of Tapestry*, London (rev. ed.), 1973.

Masterpieces of Tapestry from the 14th to the 16th centuries, Metropolitan Museum, New York, 1973.

EMBROIDERY

CLABBURN, Pamela, *Samplers*, 1977.

JOURDAIN, Margaret, 'Stoke Edith needlework hangings', *Country Life Annual*, 1951.

One Man's Samplers. The Goodhart Collection, Orleans House Gallery, London, 1983.

TOLLER, Jane, *British Samplers: A Concise History*, Chichester, 1980.

INDEX

Page numbers in *italic* refer to illustrations

Abbey Farm 29
Adam, Robert 47
'Addled' Parliament 18
Anne, Queen 48
Anne of Denmark, Queen Consort 39
Arnold, Edward 13
Arnold, Thomas 13
Arnold, William 5, 11–13, 16

Backhouse, Sir John *38*
Bacon, Francis, Baron Verulam 18
Baldwin, Stanley 31
Beach, Thomas 25
Bishopton 6
Blake, Edith (later Phelips) 20
Blunt family 11
Blyenberch, Abraham van 41, *41*
Bodiam Castle, Sussex 31
Boleyn, Anne 10
Bonar Law, Andrew 31
Bonnor, J. 85
Borlase, Sir John 39
Bridgwater, Somerset 20
Brooke family 7
Brooke Montacute, manor 7
Brounckhorst, Arnold van 35
Brown, Lancelot 'Capability' 24
Buckingham, Duke of, *see* Villiers
Buckler, John *13*, 28, 86, *88*
Burghley House, Northamptonshire 24
Burnet, Bishop Gilbert 48
Burton Agnes Hall, Yorkshire 13
Butts, Sir William 35

Canford, manor of 10
Carey, Robert, 1st Earl of Monmouth 39, *40*
Carleton, Dudley, Viscount Dorchester 39
Cartari, Vincenzo 37
Cecil, Robert, Earl of Salisbury 12
Chaloner, Sir Thomas the Elder 37
Charborough manor, Dorset 10
Charlecote Park, Warwickshire 28

Charles I, King 18, 41, *41*
Charles II, King 19
Charlton Musgrove, Wincanton 12, 13
Chastleton House, Oxfordshire 17
Chatham, 1st Earl of 22
Chessell, John 28
Christus, Petrus 34
Civil War, English 18–19, 41
Cleyn, Francis 48
Clifton Maybank, Somerset 5, 9, 10, *23*, 24
Cluniac Priory, Montacute 7, 84
Cobham, John, Lord 7
Coke, Sir Edward 11
Coker Court, Somerset 87
Coleshill, Berkshire 33
Coningsby, Sir Thomas 37, *37*
Cook, Ernest 5, 32, *32*, 33
Corfe Hubart manor 10
Corfe Mullen manor 10
Corsham Court, Wiltshire 24
Coryate, Thomas 5, 11, 14
Coventry, Thomas, 1st Baron Coventry 42, *78*
Cranborne Manor, Dorset 11–12
Critz, John de 39
Cromwell, Thomas 10
Curzon, George Nathaniel, Marquis Curzon of Kedleston 5, 13, 29, 30–1

Daillon, Jean de 44, 45
Davidson, Robert 29
Desportes, François 46, *59*
Desreumaulx, Wuillaume 44
Devereux, Walter, 1st Earl of Essex 36, 73
Dobson, William *42*, 43
Donne, Samuel 85
Dorchester House, London 26
Dorset, Earl of, *see* Sackville
Dudley, Robert, Earl of Leicester 7
Dunster Castle, Somerset 11–12, *13*

Edmondes, Sir Thomas 41
Edward V, King 34
Edward VI, King 35
Egerton, Mr 18
Elgood, George Samuel *88*
Elizabeth I, Queen 35–6, *36*, 37, 38, *39*, *74*
Elizabethan houses 14–15

'Elizabethan Revival' architecture 24, 27, 28
Essex, Earl of, *see* Devereux
Eworth, Hans 35

Fawkes, Guy 11
Ferret, Pierre 44
Fitzhardinge, Lord 20
Foley, Paul 47
Foley, Thomas 47
Fowler, John 33
Frederick V, Elector Palatine 11
Freke family 7

Gainsborough, Thomas 43
Geffray, Thomas 7
Gheeraerts, Marcus the Younger 37–8, 39, *39*
Glorious Revolution (1688) 20
Glyn, Elinor 5, 30, *30*, 31
Gobelins tapestries 46, 47, *59*
Goodhart, Douglas 48
Goodhart Collection of samplers 48–9, *48*, *49*
Gothic architecture 14
Goverson, Arnold 13
'Goverson, William' [William Arnold] 12
Gower, George 36, 37, *37*
Grey, Cecily, Dowager Marchioness of Dorset 9
Grey, Thomas, 2nd Marquis of Dorset 9
Grey family 9–10
Grimston, Edward 34
Grove, Charlotte 87
Grove, Harriet 87
Gunpowder Plot (1605) 11

Haden, G. N. & Son 28
Hall, S. C. 26, 28
Ham Hill stone 5, 14, 24
Hampton Court palace 42
Hardwick Hall, Derbyshire 14, 15, 36, 85
Harold, King 6, 7
Hastings, Battle of (1066) 6
Haynes, Bedford 13
Helyar, Ellen (later Phelips) 25–6, 27, *27*, 87
Helyar, Mrs 26, 27
Henry, Prince of Wales (d.1612) 11, 38, 39, 41
Henry IV, King 34
Henry VII, King 7
Henry VIII, King 7, 10, 34, 35, 44

Herbert, Philip, 4th Earl of Pembroke 39
Hercules tapestries 44
Hext, Sir Edward 13
Hilliard, Nicholas 35
Hippisley Cox, Geoffrey 32
Hoby, Sir Edward 37, *80*
Holbein, Hans the Younger 34–5, *35*
Holford, R. S. 26
Honthorst, Gerrit van 42, *43*
Hornby Castle portraits 34
Horsey, Sir John 9, 10, 24
Huysmans, Jakob 19

Ilchester prison escape 10
Ingilby, Cecily 27
Ingilby, Marjorie (née Phelips) 27, 28, 31, 89
Isleworth, near London 10

James I, King 11, 18, 37, 39, 41
John, King 7
Johnson, Cornelius 41–2, *42*, 42–3
Jones, Inigo 11, 39
Jonson, Ben 39, 41
Joy, T. M. *26*

Kedleston Hall, Derbyshire 30
Knight, Frank & Rutley 30
Knollys, Eardley 32
Knollys, Elizabeth, Lady Layton 36

Lanhydrock, Cornwall 13, 17
Larkin, William 39
Lee, Sir Henry 38
Lees-Milne, James 32
Leicester, Earl of, *see* Dudley, Sidney
Logor, Benedictine monk 6
Logworesbeorh estate 6
Longleat, Wiltshire 13, 85
Louis XVI, King 46
Lufton manor 7
Luttrell, George 12–13

Mary I, Queen 35
Mary II, Queen 48
Medici, Piero de' 36
Meulen, Steven van der 7, 35, *71*
Middle Temple Masque 11
Miereveldt, Michiel van 39–41
Mildmay, Carew 22

Mildmay, Edith (née Phelips) 22

millefleurs tapestry 44, 45

Monmouth, Earl of, *see* Carey

Montacute House: Clifton Maybank carvings 23, 24; Curzon's improvements 31; Edward Phelips V's improvements 5, 22–5; fenestration 15–16; garden hangings 47, 47; gatehouse (demolished) 13; inventories: 1638) 18, 19, 44, 93; (1728) 93; (1834) 25, 93; as National Portrait Gallery outstation 5, 33; parish map (1825) 86–7, 87; plans of 50–1, 92; samplers 48, 48–9, 49; stables (demolished) 88; statues of Nine Worthies 15, 16, 24; Stewart bequest 32–3, 44, 46; stone 5, 14, 24; tapestries 19, 44–8; textiles 15–16; as V & A store 32; William Phelips's plans for 26–8;
Exterior: 4, 9, 10, 13–16, 17; Approach 24, 52, 86, 87; East Front 14, 14, 15, 15–16, 52, 52, 85, 86; West Front 16, 23, 24, 28, 86;
Garden, Park and Estate: 84–91, 92; 'Banqueting House' 85; Cedar Lawn 89; East Court 13–14, 84, 88, 89–90; Garden pavilions 13, 33; Kitchen Garden 89; Lime Avenue 84, 85; North Garden 85, 87, 90, 91; West Drive 24, 86, 88, 91;
Interior: 5, 16–17; Clifton Maybank Corridor 48, 69; Crimson Bedroom 16, 44, 67–9, 68; Crimson Dressing Room 16, 67; Dining Room 44, 45, 53–5, 54, 93; Drawing Room 17, 33, 59–61, 60, 61; Great Hall 16, 17, 55–7, 57; Ground Floor Corridor (Lower Clifton Maybank Corridor) 83; Hall Chamber 16–17, 44, 47, 69; Library (Great Chamber) 11, 16, 17, 20, 44, 64–6, 64, 65, 66, 93; Library Ante-Room 63–4; Long Gallery 5, 13, 25, 33, 70–83; Lord Curzon's Bedroom 46, 62–3, 63; Parlour 17, 48, 58–9, 58, 59; Parlour Passage 57–8; Screens Passage 16, 53, 55; Staircase 45–6, 46, 61–2, 69–70

Montacute Old Park 84

Montacute parish church 91

Montacute parish map (1825) 86–7, 87

Montacute Park 84, 91

Montacute Priory 7, 84

Montacute village 6, 7

More, Sir Thomas 34, 35

Mortain, Robert, Count of 6

Mortain, William, Count of 7

Mortlake tapestry factory 48

Mountague village 6

Mytens, Daniel 41, 42

Napier, Sir Gerrard 22

Nash, Joseph 28, 28

National Portrait Gallery 5, 33

Neale, J. P. 25, 28

Neilson, James 46

Newdigate, Margaret (later Phelips) 11

Newdigate, Sir Robert 13

Ogilby, John 48

Oliver, Isaac 37

? Oudart, Nicholas 42, 43

Oudenaarde 44

Park Covert 84

Parr, Catherine 10

Peake, Robert the Elder 39

Pembroke, Earl of, *see* Herbert

Peryn, Anna 48, 48

Petre, Lord 11

Petre, Sir William 7, 7

Phelips, Ann (d.1707) 20

Phelips, Ann (née Pye) 18

Phelips, Anne 20–1

Phelips, Bartram 10

Phelips, Bridget (née Gorges) 18–19

Phelips, Bridget, Lady Napier (1707–58) 20–1

Phelips, Rev. Charles 25

Phelips, Edith (later Horsey) 9, 10, 24

Phelips, Edith (later Mildmay) 22

Phelips, Edith (née Blake) 20

Phelips, Sir Edward (1560?–1614) 5, 7, 10, 11, 12, 13, 16–18, 84

Phelips, Col. Edward (c.1613–80) 18, 19, 19

Phelips, Edward III (1638–99) 19–20, 20, 22

Phelips, Edward IV (1678–1734) 20

Phelips, Edward V (1725–97) 6, 6, 21, 22, 22, 28, 85–6

Phelips, Edward VI (1753–91) 25

Phelips, Edward Frederick (1882–1928) 31

Phelips, Elizabeth (1689–1750) 20–2, 21

Phelips, Elizabeth (née Pigott) (d.1638) 11

Phelips, Elizabeth (née Smythe) 10

Phelips, Ellen (née Helyar) 25–6, 27, 27, 87

Phelips, Emily 10

Phelips, Gerard Almarus (1884–1940) 31

Phelips, Henry 10

Phelips, Jane 7

Phelips, John (1784–1834) 17, 25, 25

Phelips, Margaret (née Newdigate) 11

Phelips, Marjorie (later Ingilby) 27, 28, 31, 89

Phelips, Richard (b.1480) 7–10

Phelips, Capt. Richard 28

Phelips, Robert (c.1613) 19

Phelips, Sir Robert (1586–1638) 18, 18, 42

Phelips, Thomas (d.1501) 7

Phelips, Thomas (c.1500–89/90) 10

Phelips, William (1755–1806) 25

Phelips, William (1823–89) 25–8, 26, 87

Phelips, William Robert (1846–1919) 28–9, 29, 31

Phelips family 5, 7, 28, 29, 32, 47, 66

Pigott, Elizabeth (later Phelips) 11

portraits: baroque 42–3; Elizabethan 35–7; Flemish 35; Hornby Castle set 34; Tudor and Jacobean 34–43

Pot, Hendrik Gerritz. 18, 18, 42

Powys, A. R. 32

Powys, Llewellyn 26, 29, 32

Pridham, Mr (gardener) 87

Pullar, Jonathan 63

Pye, Ann (later Phelips) 18

Pye, Sir Robert 18

Quelch, Mary 49

Ralegh, Sir Walter 11

Ranger's House, Blackheath 39

Ravesteyn, Jan Anthonisz. van 41

Reiss, Phyllis 84, 89

Reynolds, Sir Joshua 60

Richard II, King 34

Richardson, C. J. 16, 28, 55, 65

Rosse, Lord 33

Rowe, E. A. 89

Rubens, Sir Peter Paul 42

Rye House Plot (1683) 20

Sackville, Thomas, 1st Earl of Dorset 39

Sackville-West, Vita 32

St Catherine's parish church, Montacute 91

St Michael's Hill folly 6, 6, 24, 85–6, 91

sampler, history of 48–9

Sanderson, William 43

Scrots (Stretes), William 35

Scudamore, Lady (née Mary Throckmorton) 37–8, 39, 81

Serell, John 25

Serjeant Painters 36

Seymour, Sir Edward 10

Sherborne Abbey, Dorset 24

Ship Money 18

Shrewsbury, Earl of, *see* Talbot

Sidney, Robert, 1st Earl of Leicester 36–7, 72

'Silk Purses Ltd' 32

Smythe, Elizabeth (later Phelips) 10

Smythe, Matthew 10

Society for the Protection of Ancient Buildings 5, 32

Sock Dennis, Tintinhull 10

Somer, Paul van 39, 40

Southampton, Earl of, *see* Wriothesley

Speake, George 10

Stamfordham, Lord 31

Star Chamber 9

Stewart, Sir Malcolm 5, 32, 44, 46

Stocker, John 10

Stoke Edith, Herefordshire 47

Strong, Roy 33

Talbot, Charles, 12th Earl of Shrewsbury 20

Tattershall Castle, Lincolnshire 30–1

Taunton radicals trial (1686) 20

Throckmorton, Sir Nicholas 76

Tobias tapestries 45

Tofig, Cnut's standard-bearer 6

Tournai 44, 45

Tunbeorht, Abbot of Glastonbury 6

Tyndale, William 10

V. M., Monogrammist 38

Van Dyck, Sir Anthony 42, 43

Vere, Horace, Baron Vere of Tilbury 39, 82

Victoria and Albert Museum 32

Villiers, George, 1st Duke of Buckingham 18, 41, 42, 43

Vulliamy, Louis 26

Wadham, Dorothy 11, 13

Wadham College, Oxford 11, 12, 13

Walpole, Horace 24

Waltham Holy Cross Abbey 6

Wanstead, Essex 11

Waring, Lord 31

Wayford Manor, Somerset 11

Wentworth, Thomas, 2nd Baron Wentworth 35, 71

Westonbirt, Gloucestershire 26

Whitehall Palace 11

William of Malmesbury 6

William the Conqueror, King 6

Wollaton Hall, Nottinghamshire 14

Wolsey, Cardinal 10

Wriothesley, Henry, 3rd Earl of Southampton 39, 77

Wyatt, Sir Thomas 7

Wyatt, Sir Thomas the Younger 7

Zetland, Lord 32